DOGWINKS

Read About More Amazing Godwinks in These Books:

Godwink Christmas Stories

When God Winks

God Winks on Love

Godwink Stories

Godwinks & Divine Alignment

The Godwink Effect

The 40 Day Prayer Challenge

DOGWINKS

TRUE GODWINK STORIES OF DOGS
AND THE BLESSINGS THEY BRING

SQUIRE RUSHNELL
AND LOUISE DuART

Includes six previously published stories from Godwink series books

HOWARD BOOKS

ATRIA

New York London Toronto Sydney New Delhi

HOWARD BOOKS
ATRIA

An Imprint of Simon & Schuster, Inc.
1230 Avenue of the Americas
New York, NY 10020

CONTENTS

* This symbol denotes a story that previously appeared in another Godwinks book by SQuire Rushnell and Louise DuArt.

CONTENTS

INTRODUCTION

Is it possible that when God made dogs He was creating furry friendly agents on earth to deliver Godwink messages to people like you and me?

First, what are Godwinks?

They're "coincidences" that aren't coincidences at all, but which come from divine origin. In other words, they're person-to-person messages from God, directly to you out of eight billion people on the planet.

You've had Godwinks. Everyone has. Sometimes they are another word for "answered prayer." But not everybody has learned how to recognize them. That's one of the missions of this book. To help you identify Godwinks and find out how to get more.

Here's where dogwinks come in.

Everybody in the world knows that dogs are faithful companions. They're always glad to see you. They love you unconditionally. And they can be taught to deliver mail, newspapers, and other items.

Therefore, if you were God and you wanted to communicate Godwink messages directly to people . . . without using the spoken word . . . how would you do it?

Wouldn't you call upon your trusted canine creatures . . . that also don't use the spoken word . . . to be your Godwink links . . . the unwitting messengers of Godwinks to people like us?

That's it! You'd use dogs!

God and dog. They work as a team.

And maybe it's no coincidence that the two words are spelled with the same three letters—when you hold one up to the mirror, it spells the other (not exactly, but you get what we mean).

So, what's a book about dogwinks, and how does it help you?

Every story is an astonishing all-true Godwink story with a dog right at the center of it.

If you love dogs, you'll love every single story. Fourteen of them have never been published, while six are classics from earlier books with brand-new angles.

Some Godwink stories will make you shout "Wow!" Others will stir your heart so much you may find yourself tearing up. And then there are stories that will simply inspire you to be a better you. Dogs do that.

Every story features charming, faithful, heroic dogs, leading you to see how God's hand is working in your own life.

You'll immediately understand how God watches over you at all times, nudging you along to be at the right place at the right time to meet the people He wants you to meet, while keeping you on His GPS . . . God's Positioning System.

Something else: You'll learn to never again miss His person-to-person messages directly to you . . . His Godwinks and dogwinks.

Are you ready? Let's meet Ruby!

DOGWINKS

1

RUBY

A blue pickup truck drives into the Rhode Island SPCA parking lot, pulling into a spot adjacent to a wire fence. The sign on the truck's door, "Lazybones Dog Training," helps identify the driver.

Out hops an attractive woman in her late thirties who heads into the building. Minutes later, we see her behind the wire fence.

She is Pat Inman, a dog trainer, who donates some of her time every week to the SPCA, helping dogs get ready for their critically important adoption interviews with potential families. She teaches them basic manners. In other words, she is helping them to put their best paw forward.

"I'll be right with you, Ruby!" she shouts to her favorite

canine student, who is dashing around the enclosure. "I just need a minute to get ready."

Ruby, seven months old, is a frisky, long-haired, black-and-white pup, preoccupied with running back and forth like she's out of control.

Is she?

No, that's just the nature of Australian shepherds and border collies. Ruby's a mix of both. The breeds have nearly duplicate characteristics: very bright, highly active, and loaded with mischief.

Ruby stops, looks back to see if her friend Pat is watching. *What's this? An unguarded moment?* She bolts.

Pat, getting her long auburn hair under control for her training session, has placed her pink ballcap on the bench beside her as she pulls her hair into a ponytail.

In that moment of distraction, Ruby loops around, playfully snatches the ballcap, and zips off, carrying it in her mouth like a prize.

"Ruby! Come back here!" shouts Pat, laughing at the same time. "Ruby! Bring it here."

Ruby obeys, heading back. She likes to please Pat. Most of the time. Anybody else would have had

to chase her till exhaustion before getting that
hat back.

She trots to the bench, dropping the ballcap at
her teacher's feet. Pat good-naturedly strokes Ruby's
neck and hugs her warmly.

In her canine business, as well as her volunteer duties at
the SPCA, Pat works with dozens of dogs. She is fond of
most of them. But there's something special about Ruby.

Releasing her hug, she attempts to disguise a worry in
her heart.

Ruby is scheduled for an adoption interview later that
day. It'll be the fifth family to take her home for a "tryout."
Unfortunately, the four previous families returned Ruby
within forty-eight hours, with nearly identical complaints:
"unmanageable," "scared the children," "prone to nipping."

The last observation, "nipping," is one of the least desir-
able charges to have on a dog's record. Pat's been around
long enough to know that "nipping"—one step away from
"biting"—ignites the anxiety of lawyers. And if Ruby happens to be returned one more time, the animal shelter may
have to "make a decision." She shudders at those words.

"C'mon, Ruby," says Pat, with playful resolve in her
voice. "We've got work to do. You are going to meet some
wonderful people, so let's teach you some manners."

Pat always makes things fun. So whatever she suggests sounds good to Ruby.

If only Ruby could keep her doggie mind on what she's supposed to be doing. She gets distracted; she just can't help it.

Zip! She's off. A squirrel has entered the fenced-in area, commanding Ruby's entire attention.

Pat watches, hands on her hips, letting out a sigh.

🐾 🐾 🐾

In nearby Providence, a state police vehicle pulls into the driveway of a modest suburban home. Stepping out, handsome in his gray-and-red Mountie-like uniform, thirty-one-year-old Trooper Daniel O'Neil is greeted by Charlie, an older German shepherd.

Dan lovingly rubs Charlie's neck, asking if he's been keeping a close watch on the premises. Familiar with the question, Charlie woofs an affirmative reply.

Melissa is at the kitchen sink when Dan comes in. Their three-year-old, Gavin, runs to Daddy, who scoops the boy up, and then he leans over to his wife, planting a kiss on her cheek. Melissa smiles, grabs a towel to dry her hands, then turns to look her husband in the eyes, expressing her joy at seeing him home safe and sound.

"How you feeling?" asks Dan softly.

Melissa places her hands on her tummy. "About three months pregnant." She laughs.

"Morning sickness?"

"Not much," says Melissa. "How'd it go with you?"

Dan pulls out a chair and sits at the kitchen table, where Melissa joins him.

"Same ol', same ol'. No prospect of a partner," says Dan sadly.

Melissa knows exactly what her husband means. For several years Dan has persistently tried to get into the state police K9 unit. That's his dream. But everyone pretty much knew that without a canine partner to match up with, you'd be an officer without a purpose.

Melissa can't count the number of times Dan has made regular appointments to remain visible with Sgt. Matthew Zarrella, the canine commander for the K9 unit. He always returns home disappointed. But, bless his heart, her hubby has a trait everyone admires: he sticks to a goal like Gorilla Glue.

Melissa remembers Dan's mom telling her about her son growing up with ADD. His technique in dealing with attention deficit disorder was always to pour on the persistence. He did that in high school sports and, later, getting through the police academy. Bulldog determination.

From all of Dan's prior meetings with Sgt. Zarrella,

Melissa could recite in her sleep why there was no prospect of a partner for her husband . . . *No budget*.

"I still don't understand why canines can't be put into the state police budget." She sighs.

"They do get *put* in, they just don't *stay* in," says Dan, twisting his mouth. "Politicians look at the ten- or fifteen-thousand-dollar price tag for dogs purchased in the Czech Republic, or somewhere else in the world—especially bred for police work—and they probably freak out at what their voters might say."

"Can't they just find a nice, inexpensive rescue dog?"

"That's rare, I guess." He shrugs, then remembers something. "I was talking with Joe Warzycha—one of the top guys at Rhode Island SPCA—he says in ten years he's never had a shelter dog accepted by the K9 unit."

Melissa pats her husband's hand, smiling. "Guess we're just going to have to pray about it."

🐾 🐾 🐾

"What?" Pat Inman's heart sinks.

Joe Warzycha has just called with the news that Ruby was returned for the fifth time.

"Oh no!"

"It's worse," says Joe somberly. "Today top management

received a legal opinion that the organization is at risk. They recommend euthanasia."

"They can't do that," she pleads with Joe. "Ruby's a smart dog!"

"Pat, I feel just like you do. But they don't feel they have a choice," says Joe in sympathetic tones.

"When?" She sighs.

"Two hours," replies Joe sheepishly.

Joe hears Pat draw in a breath. He knows she is trying to regain composure.

"Ruby's being put down in two hours? I'm coming over there," says Pat briskly, then hangs up.

The blue truck pulls rapidly into the SPCA, and the familiar ponytail is bobbing under the pink ballcap as Pat marches toward Joe's office. Pat stands in front of Joe pleading for Ruby's life. "Isn't there something you can do, Joe?"

Joe shakes his head slightly and looks at her as he makes an admission. "I took Ruby home last night . . . I thought maybe I could take her. But I've got three dogs and it was like a ten-round championship fight. I had to bring Ruby back this morning. That's when I got the news from top management. I was crushed."

Pat makes her own confession. She tells him she's tried several times over the last week to convince her husband to let her bring home another dog. But he just put his foot down.

"We have four dogs and four kids, all of them with minds of their own," she explains.

Pat looks at Joe again. "We have to do something," she says plaintively. "Isn't there a K9 unit or somebody that would take Ruby?"

Joe presses his lips together, thinking about it. "The state police K9 unit has never taken one of our dogs. But . . . what do we have to lose? I know Matt Zarrella, the commander. I'll call him."

"What have we got to lose?" she repeats softly.

Pat walks out of Joe's office feeling defeated and torn. She knows the odds are against Ruby. She has to get away from there; she's done all she can. At the same time, she feels guilty. If only she could have taught Ruby some manners. On top of that, she feels badly for leaving without saying goodbye to Ruby, but she knows herself; ending up in a puddle of tears would help no one.

She climbs into the blue truck and drives slowly out of the parking lot. In her rearview mirror, Ruby can be seen scampering behind the wire fence. Not a care in the world.

Tears streak down Pat's cheeks.

Driving home, Pat vows not to come back to the shelter for a while. And she vows not to pester Joe, asking him what happened. Frankly, she doesn't want to hear what she thinks she'll hear.

For now, she concludes, *I've got to try to put that sweet dog out of my mind.*

🐾   🐾   🐾

Joe Warzycha sits quietly in his office. He wants to organize his thoughts before making the call. He draws in a deep breath and picks up the phone.

Sgt. Matthew Zarrella has been handling search-and-rescue dogs for the Rhode Island State Police for years. He started the canine unit's first search-and-rescue dog program, using dogs trained in multiple scent disciplines, and is now the K9 commander. When the call comes in from Joe Warzycha, Matt remembers him—he was with the local police department prior to going to work at the SPCA.

Joe explains that he has a dog, an Australian shepherd–border collie mix that is very smart. "Matt, would you have time to come by the shelter and take a look at her? I know she needs lots of training, but she's got drive and intelligence."

Joe is candid, explaining Ruby's history with various families who have uniformly returned the dog.

Sgt. Zarrella thinks about it. Joe sounds sincere.

Finally the commander says, "Well . . . maybe I can get over there at the end of the week."

"Sorry, Matt. That won't work. Ruby will be euthanized in less than two hours."

Matt checks the clock.

"Okay, I'm on my way."

Matt Zarrella is a former Marine whose reputation for police search-and-rescue work has gone national. His quest to work with dogs began as a boy when three Girl Scouts from Oklahoma were kidnapped on a camping trip. He kept the newspaper story on his bedroom dresser all through school, always thinking that K9 units could have found the perpetrator. He still has the article today in his office. That was the motivation for his life's work.

Matt loves dogs and has a soft spot in his tough Marine Corps heart for underdogs. He's one himself. His short stature—five-five, working among state police officers who are six feet and taller—has been a challenge all his career.

Before leaving the barracks, Matt takes two of his own search dogs from the kennel, loads them into his SUV, and heads out.

Joe is thrilled that Matt has responded promptly. He greets him, then lets him do his thing, watching from a distance. He utters a prayer, feeling satisfied that, as the good book says, "having done all, stand." He was "standing" and turning things over to a supernatural mediator to prepare Sgt. Zarrella's heart for Ruby.

During the first twenty minutes or so, Joe sees that Ruby is true to form, "unmanageable." Worse, she's aggressive toward Matt's senior female search dog.

He observes how Matt's demeanor never wavers, regardless of Ruby's behavior. And how the K9 commander studies the dog as he throws a ball, telling Ruby to get it. Over and over, Ruby chases after the ball and returns it to Matt. Joe knows that's a positive trait, demonstrating that Ruby has drive.

Joe's phone rings. He steps away to take the call, but when he returns a few minutes later, he is astonished. Matt has Ruby lying on the ground . . . and she is allowing Matt's female search dog—the one she nearly attacked earlier—to walk over her! The K9 commander is clearly finding a basis to be hopeful about Ruby.

"I'll take her, work with her, and see what we can do," says Matt. "I have a trooper in mind to pair her with."

For further evaluation, Sgt. Zarrella takes Ruby home with him for the next fourteen days.

🐾 🐾 🐾

Two weeks later Dan O'Neil can't wait to phone Melissa with the good news. Speaking excitedly, he tells her that he had been called in to meet with Sgt. Zarrella. "He said he had a partner for me! Her name is Ruby. He told me she's very smart but needs training. She's a little rambunctious."

"That's wonderful, honey."

"And listen to this, Melissa. Just like you were thinking, Ruby is a shelter dog from the RISPCA!"

Melissa is beaming on the other end of the phone. She knows this is a sign . . . an answered prayer . . . a God-wink . . . indicating that the pathway to her husband's dream is opening up.

Dan laughs exuberantly. "Honey, this is my shot!"

🐾   🐾   🐾

Ruby is glad to have the change of scenery from the animal shelter.

First, she spends a few days with Matt and his dogs . . . He plays a lot of games with her, like chasing the ball, and now she's riding in the truck with this nice man, Dan. He is talking to her all the way to . . . well . . . wherever they are going.

Melissa is waiting at the front door, holding Gavin, as Dan arrives home. Dan leads Ruby on her leash up the front steps and suddenly the pup yanks the leash out of

Dan's hand, dashing right past them into the living room. There, in the middle of the carpet, Ruby leaves her new family a present.

Melissa and Dan look at each other aghast. This is not going to be easy.

> Ruby decides to show these nice people that she is going to like living here by demonstrating her enthusiasm . . . running through the house, real fast!
>
> She feels encouraged by her cheerleader. Little Gavin laughs and laughs.
>
> Having a playmate gets Ruby even more excited. She and Gavin dash through the house together, tipping over coffee tables and wastebaskets! This place is going to be fun!

Over the next few months, making measurable progress in altering Ruby's behavior issues is frustrating. For sixteen weeks, Dan and Ruby attend a training school, working on obedience and scent detection. "It was like taking five steps forward and ten back," says Dan, partly blaming himself as an inexperienced handler. When Dan gets discouraged, he pumps himself up: *This is my only shot to be in K9, we've got to make it work.*

When Dan returns home, exhausted, Melissa is always a

source of encouragement. She reminds her husband that he and Ruby have persistence.

"You're both underdogs," she counsels, painfully aware that his colleagues at the state police barracks have been razzing him, leaving notes taped to his locker, insinuating that a shelter dog could never measure up to their bred-and-trained-for-the-job canines.

Dan keeps at it, never letting Ruby out of his sight, redundantly going through training procedures, hoping for that moment when the penny will drop. That realization that life would be better if she were obedient, rather than the opposite.

After the training school, Dan is assigned to regular police work and needs to find the time to continue training Ruby in his off-hours.

Time after time, the K9 teams are called into action searching for missing people or assisting detectives, while Dan and Ruby are left behind at the barracks, answering phones and tending to menial tasks. Alone with his dog one evening, Dan opines, "Ruby, you're the canine version of Cinderella. Everybody else goes to the ball. And here we sit."

> Ruby listens to the conversation as if she knows what Dan's talking about. *Cin-der-ella . . . wonder who she is.*

While Dan works at his desk, Ruby enjoys lying in the cubbyhole underneath, taking naps. Being in a secret-like place makes her calmer. Not to mention, she loves being right at the feet of Dan, whom she has grown to love more than anybody.

🐾   🐾   🐾

Approaching five months, Dan is suddenly starting to get glimmers of hope. Ruby is beginning to sit for five minutes without Dan holding her down.

"That was an amazing sight," he says to Melissa. "Then she started picking up on scent detection quickly and was giving me alerts." All the hard work is now paying off. After six months Ruby finally wins her certificate.

For Ruby, it is like having a hot dog dinner every day of the week. She's made it! She's got her police badge for her collar! Dan says that means they can start going on searches for missing people.

That means I've got a job? Oh boy, oh boy, oh boy!

Over the next few years Ruby has an exceptional record. She is credited with finding ten missing persons or bodies. On a cold day in October, the K9 unit is summoned to

the outskirts of Providence to search for a teenage boy who
has been missing for thirty-nine hours.

According to local police, who had searched unsuccess-
fully for two days, the boy liked to hike in the woods that
ran many miles deep behind his house.

The troopers and canines split up, each taking a segment
of the woods.

Dan gives Ruby the scent from the boy's clothing.

> Ruby begins zigging and zagging to catch the
> scent . . . The boy had walked from his house,
> crossed the lawn, down a path, into the woods,
> under brambles, over stumps, through a stream,
> up a rocky incline . . . Ruby keeps following the scent
> of the boy.

Dan is trying to keep up. It's difficult—Ruby is covering
so much territory, moving so quickly.

A mile into the woods, Ruby suddenly bolts. Dan runs
as fast as he can, trying to keep her in view.

He breathlessly arrives at a ravine. Ruby is at the bottom. She's licking the face of a prone body, trying to revive
the victim!

Dan scrambles down and turns the body over. It's a boy!
His forehead is lacerated and bloodied. He is cold and un-
conscious. His mouth and nose are clogged with blood. As

Dan searches for a pulse, Ruby begins licking the blood from the boy's mouth and nose.

Suddenly the boy takes a breath! Simultaneously, Dan feels a faint pulse.

"We have the boy, injured, lacerations to the forehead . . ." Dan speaks loudly into his radio. He then gives the others—officers, first responders, and EMTs—the GPS coordinates.

Dan takes off his jacket and covers the boy with it.

> As Dan continues to talk on the radio, Ruby takes up a position lying next to the boy to share her body heat.

"We can't find you . . ." says the voice over the staticky radio. "The GPS coordinates are off."

Dan has an idea.

> Ruby looks up as Dan gives her a command. He says, "Bark, Ruby, bark." She stands up and barks.

Dan encourages her. "That's it, Ruby, keeping barking. Good girl."

"We hear Ruby barking," says the voice on the radio. "Keep her going!"

Following the sound of Ruby, the rescuers arrive, wrap

the boy in blankets, provide him with oxygen, place him on a stretcher, carry him through the woods to the ambulance, and rush him to the hospital.

Dan and Ruby are exhausted. But they are still running on adrenaline. Before anything else, Dan has a critical task: to advise the parents that their son is alive and tell them to which hospital he has been taken.

Dan's state police truck pulls into the driveway of the boy's home.

"Stay, Ruby. I'll be back in a few minutes."

He knocks on the door. A man and a woman, with fear on their tearstained faces, invite him in. Dan knows they need good news immediately.

"Your boy is alive! My canine Ruby found him. He's going to be fine!"

"Oh, thank God!" says the boy's mother, her voice cracking. She falls against her husband as she sobs tears of joy. He's crying too.

Dan tells them their son has some injuries, but he's expected to survive. He names the hospital.

Just as Dan turns to leave, the mother calls after him.

"Officer . . . did you say your dog was named Ruby?"

Dan stops in his tracks. He turns and, with a surprised look, says, "Yes, ma'am, that's my K9 partner. The dog that just found your boy is named Ruby."

She chokes back tears. Lets out a sigh of relief.

"My name is Pat Inman, a volunteer at the SPCA. I advocated for Ruby not to be put down, hoping that the state police would take her. But I never knew what happened."

Dan is dumbfounded, his own eyes starting to moisten.

"Ma'am, that means that the dog whose life you saved just saved your son!"

Pat Inman and her husband are overwhelmed with the amazing Godwink that has just been revealed.

Dan is also astonished. He shakes his head in disbelief, takes another step to leave, then stops, and turns to say, "Would you like to see Ruby? She's in my truck."

Ruby has been climbing the insides of the truck waiting for Dan to return.

As soon as the door to the house opened, Ruby had caught the scent of her other best friend in the whole world . . . Pat!

The excitement inside Ruby is churning up and down until Dan opens the truck door. *There she is!* Ruby covers Pat in kisses the way she did when she was a little pup.

It's the best reunion that Ruby—and Pat—have ever had.

※ ※ ※

Arriving home, Dan tells Melissa every detail of the story as Ruby sits by, attentively listening. Melissa tears up, hugs Ruby. Then Dan.

They realize that supernatural forces have pulled them all together. Godwinks and dogwinks!

"You two are my underdog champions!" Melissa says with a beaming smile.

Reflections

This is the dictionary definition of "coincidence," which is a useful tool for science:

A remarkable concurrence of events without apparent causal connection.

A "Godwink" is *with* causal connection. This is its dictionary definition:

A coincidence that isn't a coincidence, but which comes from divine origin.

In the Hebrew language, the word "coincidence" doesn't exist. The rationale: if all things come from God, there is no need for the term.

When Dan and Pat realized that Ruby, whom Pat had helped save years before, had saved her son, they both knew it wasn't a coincidence. They were experiencing something of divine origin that defied enormous odds. A Godwink.

Pat Inman's son recovered fully and is attending college.

In October 2018, Ruby was named the national Search and Rescue winner in the Hero Dog Awards telecast on the Hallmark Channel.

In 2021, a two-hour movie, *Rescued by Ruby*, will premiere on Netflix.

2

SCOOTER

The scraggly black mutt with white patches, a collie mix, peeks from the cardboard container, just able to see the bottom half of a boy.

He likes little kids. They are always dropping food. A piece of candy here, the bottom of an ice cream cone there.

Cautiously, the little dog scoots from the cardboard boxes piled up behind the supermarket, his favorite place to catch a night's sleep, and rubs up against the little boy, who promptly reaches down and strokes him. *Ah, that feels good.*

The ten-year-old, wide-eyed with a hopeful smile, looked up at his dad and asked, "Can we take him home, Dad?"

His father leaned down, noted the dog had no tags or identification.

"Yeah, why not," he drawled.

Johnny Griffin couldn't remember a better day in his whole life. Sitting in the front seat looking up at his dad, his hero, with an excited new friend squeezed in between them—maybe taking his first doggie ride in a truck—what could top this?

As he thought about it, Johnny realized he now had two best friends. His new dog and his dad.

Of course, Dad was a best friend to lots of people. He was an actor who played bit parts in dozens of different TV shows. That was probably how he got into the habit of greeting friends with a warm tough-guy hug. Sometimes even a kiss on the cheek or saying, "I love you."

But, when Dad was at home, he was just Dad. A nice man who liked to express his love for people.

"What are we gonna call you, little guy?" Dad was now stroking the mutt while he drove. "Whaddya think, Johnny? You got a name for him?"

Johnny wasn't sure.

His dad then smiled. "I got an idea. Remember how this little guy scooted from those cardboard boxes? Let's call him 'Scooter.'"

Johnny grinned in agreement.

From then on, Scooter was a member of the Griffin family. The rascal lived up to his name too. His dad would build escape-proof enclosures and that inventive little mutt would always manage to scoot off. But he always came home by suppertime.

Scooter was never what you'd call a one-person dog; he was a loyal and affectionate friend to every member of the family . . . a trait he must have picked up from Dad.

🐾   🐾   🐾

On his thirteenth birthday, Johnny had no idea he was about to learn one of the biggest lessons of his life. He was sitting on the porch with six of his pals eating ice cream cones.

> Scooter lies on the porch carefully studying the boys as they eat their ice cream cones. They are talking among themselves, animatedly.
>
> Scooter hopes against hope that one of them will slip and drop his cone. He is poised . . . ready to take advantage of that misfortune.
>
> But as the boys begin to argue, elevating their voices, the little mutt tilts his head, as if to say, *Hey, hey, pipe down.*

The boys were getting into a my-dad-could-whoop-your-dad argument. It was just gathering steam when a burly Italian man strode up the sidewalk, climbed the porch steps, and knocked on the front door. The boys stopped talking as they looked the man over.

The screen door swung open and Johnny's dad burst out.

"Benny! Good to see ya!"

He then grabbed Benny, giving him a bear hug and a kiss on the cheek.

Scooter looks on as every one of the boys shifts his eyes to Johnny, like the slow burn in a movie. He sees Johnny return their looks with a tight-mouthed scowl.

Benny and Dad went in the house. Then one of the boys mockingly blurted, "Your dad's no tough guy, he's a sissy."

Johnny's reaction was instantaneous: a pop in the mouth!

Scooter jumps up onto all fours, alertly watching as things escalate into a free-for-all, with all the boys throwing punches, rolling off the porch, into the dirt, yelling dare words and swear words.

"Boys!"

A piercing, authoritative, drill-sergeant voice emanating from Johnny's petite mom brought everyone to attention. She ordered the boys to line up on the curb. Looking like bedraggled soldiers after a barroom brawl, each defendant gave his name and phone number.

"I want you to know that I'm calling each of your parents right away. Now, all of you, straight home!"

As the boys dispersed, Johnny knew he was to remain standing on the curb—alone—awaiting his fate.

His dad came out of the house wearing a tough-guy-in-the-movies face and ordered Johnny to go to the backyard and wait there for him.

> Keeping his distance, Scooter watches Johnny sweat bullets for a long time. Maybe a half hour.
>   The little dog just lies on the grass, waiting, watching, to see what will happen next.

Finally, Dad came into the yard and spoke, evenly: "Why were you guys fighting?"

Johnny stared down at his sneakers. He brushed one foot back and forth across the grass before responding.

"It's all your fault," he snapped.

Scooter lifts his body up . . . scooting a few steps
backward . . . out of harm's way.

"You kissed that guy after I was telling the guys how
tough you were," he continued.

There was a pause. A long pause. Johnny felt certain his
smart-alecky reply had just earned him a whooping as his
dad looked back at him.

Instead Dad calmly called over his shoulder to the
dog.

"Scooter, come here."

Me? You want ta talk ta me? thinks Scooter,
wondering why in the world he is being summoned.
Cautiously Scooter approaches the two.

"Sit right there, Scooter," said Dad, pointing to the grass
about ten feet from Johnny.

Looking at his son, he said, "Johnny, look at your dog
and tell him you love him."

The boy was perplexed and still embarrassed by what his
buddies had seen.

Reluctantly, Johnny said, "Scooter, I love ya."

Scooter doesn't move.

"Tell him again," said Dad.

"I love ya, Scooter," repeated Johnny, still weakly.

Scooter just sits there.

"Now," said his father, "kneel down, call the dog over, hug him, and tell him you love him."

Johnny obeyed. Kneeling down, he said, "C'mere, Scooter."

Scooter bounds to Johnny, wagging his tail and licking his face.

"Son," said Johnny's dad, grasping him by the shoulders, "love isn't something you say . . . it's something you do."

As Johnny looked into his dad's eyes, he pressed his lips together, trying to hold back the tears that were threatening to erupt.

"Humans and dogs are just alike," his dad continued. "You can tell someone you love 'em all day long, but it's when you reach out and touch them, showing affection, that's when they really know it."

Dad reached out, wrapped his arms around his son, and gave him a good, long hug. With an arm around his shoulder, Dad walked Johnny over to the picnic table and they sat down.

"Ya know, Johnny, in the Holy Bible, Jesus tells us what we need to do." He paused for a moment, then continued, "Let us not love with words or speech, but with actions and in truth."*

From that day—Johnny's thirteenth birthday—he had a new appreciation as he watched his dad live that lesson with others. And, ever since, John Griffin has practiced the lesson he learned from his dad and Scooter.

Reflections

God likes it when we live by His guiding values found in the ancient scriptures. Some have described those words, enduring for thousands of years, as God's love letter to each of us.

It stands to reason that the more we follow His biblical principles, the more He will communicate with us through His mysterious ways—Godwinks.

Sometimes, if we're fortunate, He'll communicate with the help of our pups—dogwinks.

---

* 1 John 3:18 (NIV).

3

GINGER

When Liz Pennycook's six-year-old eyes met those of the ginger-colored puppy at a local animal shelter, she knew they were meant for each other. Even though she told her mom she wanted a Dalmatian, like the ones in the Disney movie, there was something special about this puppy, a golden retriever/Irish setter/Chow mix.

If she was hesitant at all, that vanished when a man walked by and asked, as she was stroking the puppy, "What are you going to name her?" Without a moment's hesitation, Liz said, "Ginger." That sealed it. Liz and Ginger were inseparable from then on.

Throughout childhood, Ginger was part of Liz's "make-believe" play. The sweet dog sat patiently as Liz dressed her up in girly outfits, placed handmade crowns upon her head, or attached a pair of Mom's old dangly earrings. Not once could Liz ever recall Ginger growling. Her disposition was perfect.

Wherever Liz went, so did Ginger. And when Liz got her driver's license, Ginger was always eager to jump into the passenger seat, sticking her head out the window, taking in all the sights, sounds, and smells.

She must have known she was beautiful. She loved having her picture taken. Ginger would patiently pose, remaining right where Liz placed her, like a Wilhelmina model. One autumn, for instance, Liz noticed that the golden leaves on the lawn complemented the color of Ginger's soft and beautiful red coat. So, Ginger sat and took direction until the photographer (Liz) released her.

A few months later Liz noticed a small ad for a calendar company looking for dog models to grace each month of a desk calendar. She knew Ginger, with her regal look, would be the perfect calendar girl.

Liz popped into a mailing envelope that photo of Ginger among the leaves on the lawn; she smiled, lingering to take one last look at the sweet picture of her canine friend, before sealing the envelope up. It was a long shot, but Liz said a silent prayer that Ginger's photo might be chosen.

When Liz went off to college to study video production, Ginger had to stay behind with the family. On her brother's birthday in October, Liz drove four hours home from school to spend the weekend. She was so happy to see Ginger and couldn't remember another time when they had been separated for so long.

Taking Ginger for a ride in the car, with the dog's head sticking out the window, Liz sensed that her best friend was fatigued. She had no idea that Ginger was hiding a secret illness. That this would be her last earthly car ride.

Liz hated saying goodbye on Sunday afternoon. But she had to go.

The next morning at 5:30, her mom called. Ginger was fading.

Liz drove straight back home, crying the entire way. She was able to cuddle Ginger on the living room floor and be with her when she took her last breath. Liz was devastated.

For what seemed like a long time, Liz couldn't bear to release her embrace from her motionless dog. She cried and cried until she was interrupted by the sound of the doorbell.

Mrs. Pennycook came into the living room with a package. For Liz.

Liz looked confused, then opened the package. Inside was a calendar with a yellow tab on one of the pages. Liz carefully turned to that page. What she saw took her breath away. It was her beautiful picture of Ginger, surrounded by golden leaves, under the designation "Miss November, Mutt of the Month."

What a touching Godwink for Liz—the delivery of that calendar at that moment was divine alignment. A magnificent memory of her dear friend!

Reflections

When we lose a beloved pet, we ache from their absence. We feel the loss just as deeply as we would that of a human companion. God cares about all His creations and He knows how much we love our furry friends.

The good book tells us:

> *God formed every animal of the field and every bird of the sky . . . whatever man called every living creature, that was its name.** *

* Genesis 2:19 (BSB).

4

SPOTTY

I (Louise) was one of those "dorky" kids who wore saddle shoes. I was not what you'd call a social butterfly. As a matter of fact, I was painfully shy. I loved animals and felt more comfortable around my four-legged friends than the human race.

Every December, without fail, I would meticulously write out my Christmas list of presents that I wanted. At the top of the list were three big letters: DOG.

I so much wanted to have my own dog to play with and take care of. That wish was never granted. Every year my mother would emphatically say "NO!" and that was the end of the discussion until the next year.

I used to dream that I would wake up on Christmas morning and find a cuddly little puppy under the tree. I prayed so hard, but it wasn't meant to be.

I certainly understood why God didn't answer my prayer, but it still hurt and it didn't quench my desire to love a puppy.

My mother's dislike of dogs—really a fear—began when she was a little girl. Her beloved grandfather had tragically died after being bitten by a rabid dog. He had suffered a horrible death. That had left my mother devastated and gripped with fear every time she saw a dog.

One day I made the mistake of asking one more time. She was having an extremely stressful day. Her nerves were frayed, and on top of that she was dealing with a migraine headache. She suddenly blurted out, "The only way you are going to get a dog is if somebody leaves it to you in their will!"

Gulp. I felt a lump in my throat as I held back tears. I never asked her again.

God did give me a partial answer to my prayer, though. Our former tenant Bill Stellberger had an elderly mother who needed a dog-sitter. Even though I was only twelve years old, Bill knew I would be the perfect person to fit the bill.

Mrs. Stellberger had the smartest and most wonderful dog named Spotty. She was a mix of cocker spaniel and border collie. We hit it off immediately, and it was love at first sight for both of us.

Every time I would step foot in Mrs. Stellberger's house, Spotty would leap into my arms and lick my face, crying with delight at seeing me. I cherished the time we spent to-

gether and felt such sadness when I had to leave. I counted
the days until I would see her again.

One day just before Christmas, Bill knocked on the
door and told us the sad news that his mother had passed
away. He then disclosed that his mother had left me something in her will.

Me? Why me? I wondered. I wasn't a member of the
family.

"I need to get it. It's in the car," he said, turning from
the doorway.

Mom and I watched as Bill went to his car and opened
the door.

Out jumped Spotty! She made a beeline for me, wrap-
ping her forelegs around me, and she could hardly contain
herself.

With tears in my eyes I thanked Bill profusely, but I
knew my mother's stand on dogs. I was frozen in time and
didn't want the lovefest to end.

Out of the corner of my eye I looked up at Mom. She
had a blank look on her face.

*Does she remember what she once said—the only way I'll
get a dog is if it's in somebody's will? What if she doesn't remember . . . and says no? Will I ever see Spotty again?*

I tentatively looked up at her, mustering the courage to
whisper, "Ma . . . can I keep her?"

She didn't answer.

I could feel the tears welling up and my face flushing.

It seemed like a lifetime. Her strained response finally came. "Yeah. I guess I don't have much of a choice!"

I never felt such joy! I couldn't stop crying happy tears. Spotty was mine! Mine! God had given her to me! My life was complete!

Every day I spent with my precious friend was pure joy. She would wait for me, looking out the front window, tail wagging, anticipating my return from school. We were inseparable. I never felt such unconditional love. (Not until I met SQuire, of course!)

My mother eventually fell in "like" with Spotty and her fear of dogs slowly went away. God gave me the desire of my heart and answered my prayer in the most unexpected way. It was the most wonderful Godwink I ever received.

Spotty lived to be seventeen. She was my best friend and my confidante. When the dreaded time came that we had to put her to sleep, it was the saddest day of my life.

To this moment I can't think about my sweet Spotty without tearing up. I know in my heart that I will see her again. I can picture her now, waiting for me at Heaven's gate—just as she did in the front window of our old house—tail wagging and ready to jump into my arms again.

Until then, SQuire will have to do!

Of course, I'm being facetious about SQuire, but those of you who have pets know that some of the greatest gifts and deepest joys that God gives us come in furry packages. Spotty wasn't a gift that came in a box. But as Mom and I stood on the doorstep that day, Spotty sure became my best Christmas gift ever!

Reflections

Was there ever something that you wanted more than anything, and you prayed for it, but knew there was no earthly way that God could possibly answer your prayer? Never lose faith. Prayer is your most important connector to the desires of your heart.

The more you communicate with Him—through prayer—the more He'll communicate back to you through Godwinks, which, after all, is another word for "answered prayer."

We often paraphrase a famous evangelist, Sir William Temple, from the 1650s:

When I pray, Godwinks happen,
and when I don't, they don't. *

---

* Temple, William: "When I pray, coincidences happen, and when I don't, they don't"; https://www.brainyquote.com/quotes/william_temple_153685, accessed April 19, 2020.

5

RECKLESS

They were getting scared.

From the porch of their New Jersey home, Chuck, Elicia, and their three children watched as the angry Atlantic Ocean, the distance of a couple of football fields away, pounded the shoreline and dunes. Hurricane Sandy's winds were becoming fiercer by the minute.

"Shouldn't we go?" said Elicia with mounting worry in her voice.

"Yeah. Everything's in the car."

"Johnny's equipment and all the attachments?"

"Yeah. We're set."

Johnny, a nearly-four-year-old special-needs child, required a feeding tube, powered by special equipment.

"I also put out plenty of water and food for Reckless," Chuck continued.

"Can't we take Reckless?" asked Emily, the middle child.

"I'm sick about it," said Elicia sadly, "but every shelter told us, 'No pets allowed.'"

Emily quietly began to cry as her older sister, eight-year-old Isabella, comforted her.

"He'll be okay, honey," Elicia said, as reassuringly as she could.

"He'll be good. He's strong," Chuck agreed, adding with a sense of urgency, "C'mon, guys. One last goodbye to Reckless," as they all scrambled up the stairs to the second floor of their two-story home.

> Reckless, surrounded by a spaghetti pot filled with water and three bowls of dog food, is suddenly confused as the family swarms around him, petting him, saying, "Goodbye, goodbye, goodbye."

Chuck patted Reckless on the head, giving a slight tug to the collar with his name on it, just to be certain it was securely attached. "We'll be back tomorrow to get you, Reckless." At least that was the plan.

The kids each hugged the muscular American pit bull mix.

Elicia stroked his dark tan fur, running her fingers over the white markings above his eyes, and the tiny scar that Reckless had had since he was a pup.

Reckless is liking all the attention. But he wonders,
Are we all going somewhere?

The calm before the storm was over. A police car rushed by on the beach road, loudspeakers blaring, "Get out . . . get out now! The dunes have broken!"

Elicia jumped up, shouting, "Come on. Let's go!"

The kids were sobbing as they shouted "Bye, Reckless" over their shoulders as they were being hustled downstairs and out to the van.

Chuck was conflicted for a moment. Should he leave the bedroom door closed or open, letting Reckless have the run of the house?

He compromised, leaving it open just a crack.

Reckless runs to the window, putting his paws on
the sill, looking out, seeing the storm lash the shore
as the family van drives away.
    He barks several times. But nobody hears him.

As Chuck pulled the minivan from the driveway, he realized they were in trouble. A foot or more of water was already covering the road.

The streetlights were not working, and dark storm clouds plunged the family into pitch darkness.

Rain was beating down on the van as the windshield

wipers struggled to keep up with their mission. Chuck drove blindly, hoping he was still on the road. Soon the water was inching above the car's headlights.

Elicia shouted, "Everyone pray! God, please save us!"

They went through another several minutes of terror, totally in God's hands, as they approached higher ground and the van finally began to get more traction on the street.

The kids became more and more worried about leaving Reckless by himself.

"If I have to swim home tomorrow, I'll go back to check on Reckless. Okay?" Chuck promised as he leaned over the steering wheel, trying to make out where they were so they could get to the shelter.

> An animal has basic fight-or-flight instincts. The moment they perceive they are under attack, their nervous system triggers a rush of adrenaline to prepare them for fighting or fleeing.
>
> Reckless can see and smell a difference in the air as the hurricane barrels into New Jersey. He instinctively determines that fleeing is the best option. He runs to the door. It is open just a little. He pushes it open, then dashes downstairs, running from the front room to the kitchen. There is no way out, no way to flee.

The rain is now beating down on the house with
fierce winds. He runs back and forth, looking for a
way to get out. Suddenly he is standing in water!
The water is in the house, covering the entire first
floor!

Reckless swims to the stairs and climbs back
up to the second-floor bedroom, drinking some
water, eating a little dog food, then curling up under
the bed, as protection, from the winds and rain
battering the windows and the roof.

Arriving at the school shelter, Chuck and Elicia covered
the children as best they could, quickly carrying them inside, but it was impossible not to get drenched. Looking
bedraggled, Chuck went back to park the van and bring
in the bag Elicia had packed with essentials. He thought
about bringing Johnny's feeding tube mechanism, but it
was much too complicated at the moment. He decided to
first get to safety and let the hurricane settle down.

After a sleepless and uncomfortable night in the shelter,
at daybreak Chuck and three other men ventured outside
to take a look. There was just moderate rain, and the winds
had subsided. But the wreckage from the storm was everywhere.

Thank goodness the van was still intact. Chuck carried

the machine and equipment for Johnny's feeding tube into the shelter.

By afternoon they were told that shoreline waters had receded sufficiently for them to attempt to return home to survey the damage.

The kids were excited. They could check on Reckless.

> Looking from the upstairs window Reckless can hear the van before he can see it. Then it appears, carefully making its way around debris in the road.
>
> He becomes more and more excited as the van turns into the drive. His tail begins to wag rapidly.
>
> Soon he is dashing down the stairs to greet the family coming through the door!

"Reckless!" shouted a chorus of children's voices as the dog danced around, greeting each member of the family.

There was little doubt that they were all so grateful that Reckless made it through Hurricane Sandy. But their house didn't fare as well.

Chuck and Elicia were shocked. The entire first floor was covered in soggy mud. Not a single piece of furniture was upright, nor did it look like anything could be salvaged.

"I'm heartsick," said Elicia, looking around. "We can't stay here, Chuck. This place is uninhabitable."

A confused and worried look on his face, Chuck looked around and sighed. "Nobody could live here, hon. This place is going to have major mold problems. Everything has to be stripped and thrown away."

"What do we do?" asked Elicia plaintively.

Chuck thought a moment. Then he shrugged. "Go back to the shelter, I guess. Hopefully FEMA will show up with housing alternatives."

When an area is officially declared a disaster, the Federal Emergency Management Agency provides assistance for victims.

"Let me see if there's anything salvageable," said Elicia. "Why don't you and the kids take Reckless outside."

Trying to keep the kids distracted from the destruction, which was in evidence everywhere, Chuck made a game out of picking up debris in their fenced-in backyard. Reckless joined in on the fun.

> Dancing happily around the kids, Reckless is thrilled to get out of that house that shook through the night.
>
> A dog's first order of business, built in, is to take care of nature. Having completed that task, he can't wait to engage in one of a dog's favorite activities—fetching sticks tossed by the kids.

Isabella tosses a stick across the yard to a place right by the wire fence. Reckless runs so fast he bumps into the fence, which, weakened by the storm, separates from the post.

A dog's curiosity is also built in. An escape route is presenting itself. Who could resist? He glances back. The kids are now playing tag with their dad.

Reckless presses into the opening and immediately comes to a halt. His head is stuck, his collar caught on the wire fence. He pushes. Pushes harder. Snap! The collar breaks, the fence separates, and he finds himself on the other side.

Reckless looks through the fence. The kids are now chasing each other as Chuck picks up things in the yard.

Before he even realizes it, Reckless is responding to an internal call for adventure—to run away— to see where the trail from home takes you.

"Let's go, Chuck," said Elicia, who came out of the house into the yard. "I'm sick to my stomach—nothing can be saved. Nothing!" She was biting her lip to prevent showing tears in front of the children.

"Okay, kids, let's get in the van," said Chuck dejectedly, looking around for their dog.

"Where's Reckless? Did he go back in the house?" he asked his wife.

"No . . . the door's closed," she said, looking around.

"Oh no!" Chuck saw the loose fence, Reckless's collar stuck to it. He gazed around, looking for their pet. But he wasn't anywhere to be seen.

"Reckless escaped! The fence must have been damaged by the storm."

"Reckless! Reckless!" Chuck and Elicia called from the open windows of the van as they slowly drove up one street and down another, all through their neighborhood.

The children cried and worried about their dog all the way to the shelter. In their prayers as they went to bed that night, and for weeks thereafter at their temporary hotel, they asked for Reckless to come back.

Making things worse for the family, the company that Chuck worked for was wiped out by Hurricane Sandy. He therefore needed to spend a good part of each day looking for work. But he also devoted a portion of time to searching for Reckless, keeping his promise to the children that he would never give up.

He developed a route, from shelter to shelter, checking in with different agencies and rescues, always hoping to discover that Reckless had been picked up and checked in.

As the months wore on, finding a job was far more challenging than Chuck could have imagined. Yet, at the end of each day, returning to their temporary quarters, he knew the kids would not be asking about his success in finding work; instead they would ask, "Daddy . . . did you find Reckless?"

🐾 🐾 🐾

Reaching the first anniversary after Hurricane Sandy, Chuck and Elicia still couldn't return to their home. Chuck was able to find occasional construction jobs but still didn't have a steady income. And the children's sense of loss about their missing dog was just now starting to fade into memory.

Isabella's tenth birthday was coming up. Elicia had an idea, but wasn't sure how Chuck would feel about it: to adopt another dog—to finally fill the hole in the hearts of the children left by Reckless.

Chuck liked the idea. But they both wanted it to be a surprise. So, after the kids went to school, they visited an animal rescue agency. What they were told disappointed them. They couldn't qualify as an adoptive family because their boy was still under five years old.

Chuck reassured his wife that he was sure they could find a way to succeed with their mission of joy for Isabella and the other kids.

He made a few calls, then excitedly told Elicia, "Good news. The Monmouth SPCA doesn't have an age minimum for children. Let's go there."

Chuck and Elicia walked into the SPCA. They liked it immediately. The dogs were not in cages. Instead, along both sides of the walls, there were glassed-in spaces, about the dimensions of a typical shower stall, each housing a different dog.

As Chuck came to the first window, he was amused. "Hey. This guy looks just like Reckless. Just a little heavier."

Elicia was looking at another resident on the opposite wall. She turned to see what Chuck was talking about.

"Doesn't he look like Reckless?" He laughed.

Elicia gazed at the dog for a moment. Then she shouted, "That *is* Reckless!"

"Naw," said Chuck in disbelief.

"Yes, it is. Look at that scar on his head!"

Chuck looked and his eyes widened. "Can we see this dog, please?" he said excitedly to the SPCA volunteer.

Moments later Reckless was wagging his tail and jumping up and down.

The volunteer couldn't figure it out. She watched as the dog on her leash danced in circles.

Reckless couldn't believe it. He wanted to say, "Hey,
guys! Where have you been?!"

He's been waiting and waiting. Every day for
almost a year. And the day of his dreams has finally
arrived!

On the way back to their hotel, Chuck and Elicia
planned it all out. She'd go into the room, get the kids arranged on the sofa, and tell Isabella that her birthday present
was about to be delivered, but that the littler kids needed to
promise to help her take care of her present. They all agreed.

Elicia cracked open the front door and said, "You can
bring in the present now."

Chuck and Reckless came through the door. The children squealed!

Wow! Reckless has never been more excited in his
life!

Here are his kids! Oh, how he has missed them!
He dances again and again.

This was the best moment the whole family had experienced in a year.

It was a hurricane-sized Godwink dogwink!

Reflections

When we go through times of trouble—hurricanes, tornadoes, pandemics—Godwinks and dogwinks are delivered
to us out of the blue, as faith-building spirit-lifters.

After a long period of personal and financial hardships,
the return of Reckless was the best birthday gift Isabella
ever received, and one that Chuck, Elicia, and the kids will
never forget.

As for Reckless, the ageless spiritual says it best . . .
"I once was lost but now am found."*

---

* "Amazing Grace," American hymn, public domain, www.hymnal.net/en/hymn
/h/313.

6

BULLET

Every creature is divinely aligned with others—mysteriously, auspiciously, often unknowingly—and only later can we see the invisible threads that connected us, causing us to be exactly where we were supposed to be to fulfill our destiny.

This is the true story of a dog and two women—Pam and Ann—whose lives were woven together by a golden retriever named Bullet.

April 2001—Bellport Animal Hospital, Bellport, Long Island

"Good boy," said Dr. Laurence Cangro, gently stroking the head of Bullet, a favorite patient for thirteen years.

"Will he be okay?" asked Pam anxiously, choking back tears.

The vet paused and replied gently, "I'm afraid I don't have good news. First, I don't like the sound of his heart. Second, Bullet's enzyme levels are elevated . . . an indication of cancer of the liver, which golden retrievers are prone to get."

Pam rapidly drew in a breath and squeezed the arm of her husband, Troy.

"I need to check the ultrasound results. May I leave you and Bullet for a few minutes?" The doctor looked kindly at both of them, said he wouldn't be long, then left the room.

Pam Sica, early forties, was holding back tears. She had somehow fooled herself into thinking this day would never come.

She had always told people, "Bullet is my child, my shadow. I see into his soul and he sees into mine." But now she was gazing into the eyes of her best friend forever; he was motionless, barely capable of staying awake, lying on a cold stainless-steel table at the vet's office.

With her lower lip quivering, Pam leaned in, face-to-face with Bullet, her brown eyes locking with his, speaking a secret language they'd spoken so many times before, communicating how much they loved each other.

Bullet wants to show his love for Pam by kissing her
right on the face, and nuzzling her neck, just the way
he's done since that very first day in the puppy pen.
The moment he saw her, a deep instinct said: *She's
mine. Nobody else's.* And he ran past all the other
puppies to get to her.

"Bullet," she whispered, "you know I've loved you from
the very first day I saw you. I called to the other puppy, the
one I'd picked out earlier, but he wouldn't come to me. Instead you bounded over, looked me right in the eyes—like
now—as if to say, *Hey, pick me! Take me home!* I know that
I didn't pick you . . . you picked me!"

Dr. Cangro returned.

Pam stood up and clung to Troy.

The doctor took a breath, then calmly spoke in mea-
sured tones: "The ultrasound clearly shows that Bullet has
a cancerous tumor on his liver. But we are catching this
early—there's a chance we can save Bullet. But I want you
to think about it overnight."

Pam caught her breath, squinching up her face to keep
from crying.

"The first thing to consider is Bullet's age. He's getting up there. The average retriever lives eleven to twelve
years . . . and he's already beyond that."

Pam let out a small crying sound.

"Secondly, it's expensive."

There was a pause. Troy felt it his responsibility to ask, "Do you have a ballpark, how much?"

"About $5,000."

Dr. Cangro reiterated, "Why don't you think about it . . . sleep on it. And call me tomorrow."

She didn't want to leave Bullet, but Pam realized she had no choice. She leaned over and kissed him on the head. "Rest well, Bullet. I'll see you tomorrow."

Troy rubbed Bullet's neck.

> Bullet tries, but he can't lift his head. He doesn't understand Pam's words, but he can feel her heart . . . She and Troy are wrestling with something that is making them sad. That makes him sad too. At this moment, though, he doesn't have the energy even to keep his eyes open.

Troy, feeling a lump the size of a golf ball in his throat, wrapped his arms around Pam and led her out of the vet's office. He was glad he could be there for his dear wife; he couldn't imagine how she could have handled this on her own. He was an air traffic controller, and this, auspiciously, happened to be his day off.

As he opened her door to the car, Pam looked up at him with begging eyes and whispered, "Troy, how can we possibly afford it?"

As they drove from the animal hospital, Pam let out the tears she'd been holding inside, all that time.

Later That Same Day—Orlando, FL

Ann Givens, a twenty-eight-year-old reporter with the *Orlando Sentinel*, was excitedly tapping her fingers on the steering wheel of her little red Honda Civic. She was calling her fiancé, Rafer Guzman, a staff reporter for the *Wall Street Journal*, but he didn't seem to be picking up.

"Hi!" Rafer finally answered, sounding a little out of breath.

Ann flashed a warm smile, her hazel eyes lighting up a sweet face framed with shoulder-length brown hair. "Where've you been?" she chided him jokingly.

"Sorry I couldn't take your call earlier. I was in a meeting with my editor. Did you get it?" asked Rafer eagerly.

She paused for suspense.

"Yes!" she said, with a giggle in her voice.

"Really?"

"You are now talking to the next cub reporter to take

on the world . . . from the pages of *Newsday*. 'Your Eye on LI'!" She laughed at herself as she quoted the Long Island newspaper's slogan.

"That's amazing. When do you start?"

"In four weeks."

"That's the best news I've heard all day. I can't wait to see you!"

April 2001—Bellport, Long Island

Pam and Troy lived in an L-shaped ranch house on a quiet street of well-kept, modest homes, located on the south shore of Long Island.

Bullet's survival was one of the weightiest decisions of their lives. Pam couldn't stop crying, or reiterating, "He's my child, my shadow."

They talked to family members as Dr. Cangro had suggested. Pam's mother; her dad and stepmom in Florida; Troy's mom; and others. Everyone knew the special relationship between Pam and Bullet, and conveyed their expressions of sadness. Ever so gently, each raised the question of prudence—spending that kind of money on a dog who, if he survived the surgery, had already exceeded the average life span.

Exhausted from crying nonstop, Pam said, defeatedly, "I don't want to think about this anymore tonight."

"That's a good idea. You need to get some rest now. Sleep on it," Troy said.

🐾 🐾 🐾

At the vet's office in the morning, Pam and Troy asked for a few minutes together with Bullet.

Pam placed her forehead against Bullet's. Her golden retriever lay motionless on the table.

"I don't know, Troy. I still don't know," she said, her voice cracking. "He's my baby."

Troy placed a hand on Pam's shoulder. He had already told her he would support anything she wanted to do.

Then, as she had so many times in the past, Pam put her face right up close to Bullet's. He opened his eyes. Looking deeply into each other's eyes, they seemed to communicate in a wordless language. There was a moment of silence.

Then, Pam turned to Troy. Looking more composed, she said, "I think . . . Bullet is telling me . . . 'I'm not ready to go. I have more to do.'"

Pam and Troy found a way to borrow the money and told the doctor to please schedule the surgery.

A few days later Dr. Cangro reported that Bullet came through his surgery with flying colors. He was released forty-eight hours later.

Bullet walked beside Pam and Troy, a little more slowly than usual, out of the Bellport Animal Hospital.

"We're going home, Bullet!" said Troy, holding the leash. "Dr. Cangro says you did very, very well. He's happy."

They reached the minivan. Pam leaned down and held Bullet's face with two hands. "And only God knows how happy I am! When we get home, we're going to celebrate with a steak." She smiled and tousled his fur as Troy lifted Bullet into the back seat.

> Bullet liked that word "home." And the other one . . . "steak."

Summer 2001—Melville, NY

Newsday, one of the metropolitan New York area's most respected daily newspapers, is located in Melville, about forty minutes from Brooklyn. The paper covers Long Island news as well as relevant stories about New York City.

Ann and Rafer's Brooklyn apartment was conveniently located between their two jobs: Rafer's daily subway commute to Manhattan, and Ann's forty-minute drive to *Newsday*. That left her with her car available for assignments.

As a cub reporter, she had a beat covering the news from the Long Island towns—police actions and fires, Town Hall meetings, and occasionally a human-interest story about one of the community's characters.

"Don't expect anyone to hold your hand," one of the editors told her flatly. "Show up with your pad, pencil, and map." In other words, don't expect the newspaper to sharpen your pencils or tell you how to get somewhere on Long Island. You're on your own, so be resourceful.

During those early months Ann grew to respect the many distinguished journalists who worked for *Newsday*. Despite what that editor said, most would offer kind counsel to their younger colleague.

As the summer rolled on, she loved being reunited with Rafer and was enjoying her job, although the mundane coverage of small-town squabbles and local politics never had the potential of getting her byline anywhere close to the coveted front page.

September 9, 2001—Bellport, Long Island

"How old is Bullet now?" asked the neighbor taking her sunrise walk as Troy and Pam were piling the last things into the car for the drive to Florida.

"He's fourteen," Pam said, and smiled. Then, tousling his fur, added, "A little less energy, but still tickin'."

"We'll keep an eye on things while you're away. Say hello to your dad." The neighbor waved as she watched Pam help Bullet into the back seat. Soon the minivan was loaded up and heading down the street.

The thirty-six-hour drive to the center of Florida was one they'd done before. Of course, they could have gotten deals on flights, but Pam insisted that Bullet accompany them everywhere possible. So leaving him behind, or putting him in the baggage hold of an airplane, was out of the question.

As Troy and Pam drove, they talked about the new boat they'd recently bought. Troy was thrilled, saying the boat glided on water when they took it for a spin a couple of weekends before. "It has nice maneuverability," he observed as they made their way down I-95.

"If you say so. I still can't figure why that boat made me seasick. That never happened with the old boat," said Pam.

Troy, always one to analyze things, thought about why that would happen, then shrugged. "I really don't know. Maybe it wasn't the boat; maybe it was something you ate." Then, wanting to include Bullet in the conversation from his spot in the back seat, Troy said loudly, "What do you think, Bullet? You're always tuned in to your best pal."

> Bullet doesn't have a comment. He appreciates the thoughtful gesture of including him, but ever since Troy put the window halfway down at the last rest stop, he has been as happy as a dog off the leash to be sitting there letting the fresh air blow through his fur.

On Monday evening, Pam and Troy were looking a little more tanned, thanks to their first full day at Disney World, ten minutes from the Kissimmee home of Pam's dad, Luddy, and her stepmom, Carolyn. Even though Pam was feeling tired, they had an Animal Kingdom visit planned for the next day.

In the kitchen, preparing for dinner, Pam caught Carolyn looking at her. "Are you okay?" her stepmom asked.

Pam replied dismissively, "I'm just a little tired . . . all that sun."

"Are you feeling sick in any way?"

"No, not really. The other day Troy and I were out in his boat. I was feeling a little seasick . . . but honest, I'm fine now."

"You've been craving sweets," countered Carolyn, perceptively. "Maybe you're pregnant."

"Ha! After all this time?" At forty-two, Pam had a history of four miscarriages. Following the last one, seven years ago, her doctor had said pregnancy was "highly unlikely." She shrugged and told Carolyn, "I've stopped thinking about having a baby."

After dinner Carolyn ran out to do some errands. When she returned, Pam and Troy were already in their room. Knocking on the door, she handed Pam a box: a pregnancy test kit.

Pam smiled with a twisted mouth and scoffed, "You're wasting your money, Carolyn!"

The next morning Pam was up before sunrise. She went into the bathroom, saw the box, and took the test.

Moments later she was jostling her husband. "Troy, Troy! How would you like a little souvenir of Florida?"

He blinked at her questioningly.

"I took the test . . . I'm pregnant!"

His jaw dropped in disbelief. He laughed and pulled her to him.

Bullet joins in on the excitement. He picks up the empty box from the tester and begins running around the room, then into the living room, and through the kitchen. Although not sure what they are celebrating, the puppy in him is never too far beneath the surface.

A Short While Later . . .

Bullet is resting under the kitchen table, enjoying all the upbeat conversation and loving the smell of bacon. Over the sounds of the TV playing in the living room, he can detect an unusual brightness in all the chatter. And every once in a while a hand appears with a shared treat. This is such a great day!

Pam and Troy, in joyful expectation, traded aspirations with Pam's dad and stepmom. Would it be a boy or girl . . . did it matter? Would he or she be an air traffic controller like Troy when they grew up? . . . A player for the Mets? . . . Or work in the hospitality business like Pam? Again, they allowed themselves the dream of raising a family, dusting away all disappointments of the past.

"I just have the sense that God is going to bless this baby

in ways we can't imagine," said Pam hopefully. Her father and stepmother nodded; they themselves were getting excited about another grandchild.

Troy, always madly in love with his wife, particularly loved seeing her exuding enthusiasm. He knew that this dream come true would be an enormous gift at this time of their lives.

Luddy had gotten up from the table and walked into the living room. He shouted, "Troy—you better call work! Come look at this!"

The four of them stood transfixed at the TV. They were riveted in horror as the television images showed an aircraft flying into one of the two World Trade Center buildings in New York.

Not long after, they were stunned, along with the rest of the world, as a second plane crashed into the second tower. Now they knew it wasn't an accident. This was an act of war. And they watched the unimaginable as both buildings—world landmarks representing the towering strength of America—collapsed into rubble.

Troy had special telephone access to his work as an air traffic controller. He called his boss to see if he was needed. Whoever answered the phone was in such crisis mode, they instantly hung up.

Pam quietly became more and more anxious. Like a

brightly colored birthday balloon, she felt punctured as the joy for the new life within her slowly drained from her psyche, converting into enormous anxiety. All the excitement and optimism of bringing a baby into the world was now turning on the question: *What kind of world am I bringing my baby into?*

Same Time, Same Day—Brooklyn

Ann was calling the *Newsday* office from her apartment. The TV was on in the background with the video of the first plane crashing into the World Trade Center being played over and over.

"Okay," she repeated into the phone with a sense of urgency. "I'll get to the base of the Brooklyn Bridge and gather interviews from victims walking off." She paused as the person she was speaking to asked a question. Then she answered: "The bridge is four miles from my apartment."

Not long after, holding her notebook, Ann gazed at the stream of frightened and weary people coming off the bridge. Her heart went out to the dozens of people covered in white ash, like a scene out of a horror movie, walking toward her almost zombie-like. Some were too shocked even to speak. Others talked loudly, seemed to need to tell their stories in great detail.

For hours she interviewed people crossing over the Brooklyn Bridge, stopping every once in a while to call the paper with her notes.

Often the cell service didn't work and Ann had to stand in a long line at a pay phone.

When Ann arrived at *Newsday* the following morning, it was surreal. Instead of it being a boisterous war room, as one might imagine, people were introspective and quiet; it was as though the events of the past twenty-four hours were so tragic and horrendous, no one wanted to dwell on them in idle chatter. Everyone went on with their jobs as efficiently and as quickly as they could.

September 16, 2001—Kissimmee, FL

Five days after 9/11, Troy had connected with colleagues at work and confirmed that bridges and tunnels in and out of New York had been reopened. He and Pam packed up their minivan, put Bullet into his seat, and left at dawn Sunday on their journey back up I-95 from Florida to New York in order for Troy to be back at work on Tuesday. They were glad to be heading home.

During the trip Bullet can sense the undercurrent of anxiety . . . with Troy and Pam . . . and everyone, even people at the rest stops. He is most content sitting in the back seat, window down, inhaling the salty scent of the warm sea breezes, hearing different sounds and birds, and picking up the scents of autumn approaching as they travel north.

He muses about their vacation. And the new joy in Pam's voice when she talks about the . . . What does she call it? The "baby."

As Troy and Pam drove, they witnessed an extraordinary sight. Flags were flying everywhere. From buildings and homes and dangling from every crane at every construction site. Each flag seemed to be shouting a defiance against an enemy that would not defeat us, but make us stronger and united Americans.

They were quiet as they approached the skyline of New York. A large column of smoke rose from the devastation in Lower Manhattan. Once they passed over the Verrazzano-Narrows Bridge heading toward Long Island, they knew they were only an hour or so from home in Bellport.

The Next Week—*Newsday* Offices, Melville, NY

Ann and many other reporters were given assignments that would become their daily tasks for months to come. In addition to their usual beats, they were asked to research and write one or two obituaries—personal stories about victims identified in the carnage—with a large portion of their day spent hearing the heartbreaking stories of loved ones who had died.

Newsday developed a daily section called "The Lost" to memorialize those who had perished. It turned out to be a source of great comfort for thousands of readers.

Early 2002—Bellport, Long Island

Pam continued working at her job in the hospitality business, trying her best to separate the horrendous events of 9/11 from the wonderful news that she had received on the same day. Doctors calculated that the baby was conceived during July 2001 and that full-term birth would be in late April 2002.

She grew more and more excited as she felt the baby moving within her, holding on to the belief that she articulated that morning she discovered her pregnancy. She

honestly believed, this time, things would be different . . .
no more miscarriages . . . God's blessing would be realized.

Still, she remained cautious, never taking unnecessary
chances, getting her sleep, and always following her doctor's advice.

In her third trimester Pam's gynecologist advised that
she was suffering from placenta previa, an abnormality that
occurs in 1 of 200 births. Her doctor prescribed bed rest as
the primary treatment, and told Pam that placenta previa
nearly always requires cesarean delivery.

> Bullet senses something different going on—Pam's
> body has been changing in size and she'll hold his
> head next to her belly, letting him listen to the tiny
> sounds going on inside her. Every once in a while
> he feels little movements; they startled him at first,
> then made him curious. This much he knows: this
> thing Pam calls "the baby" is something he likes.

April 10, 2002

Baby Troy was born about two weeks early at Stony Brook
University Hospital, thirty minutes from their home. Because the baby's birth was considered complicated, and due

to Pam's cesarean delivery, she and the baby were required to remain hospitalized for four days.

Pam was concerned about Bullet being home alone and mentioned it to a Stony Brook nurse. The nurse had an idea, returning with one of the hospital blankets that had swaddled baby Troy. "Have your husband give this to your dog. It may give him comfort to smell the baby, but also prepare him for when the baby comes home," she advised.

Troy would show up at the hospital in late afternoon to visit Pam and the baby. He was soon bringing amusing and heartfelt stories of Bullet and the baby blanket.

"He drags that blanket everywhere," said Troy, laughing at the images in his mind. "He sleeps with it, runs around the house with it; he even takes it outdoors when he has to do his business."

Pam laughed too. "I guess Bullet is comforted. Me too!"

April 2002—Brooklyn

Offering Ann a modicum of escape from her daily obituary writing was the bright light at the end of the tunnel of summer—Labor Day—when she and Rafer were going to be married in a park near the Brooklyn Bridge. It wasn't to be a large wedding, but just talking about it and planning it provided relief from the dark cloud that hung over every newsroom in the country, and especially those in metro-politan New York.

April 14, 2002—Stony Brook University Hospital

Pam was thrilled when they said she and her baby could finally go home, even though the baby had breathing dif-ficulties.

"I can't wait for you to meet Bullet," she cooed to baby Troy, strapped into his car seat, in the back.

Speaking to Troy as he drove, she asked, "Do we have anything to eat in the house? I'm starved."

Troy said that he'd gotten a few things at the store and reported that the baby's bassinet was set up right next to Pam's side of the bed, just as she'd asked.

"Whatever we do, let's try to get to sleep early," she sug-gested. Troy nodded.

Woof, woof, woof.

Bullet isn't usually much of a barker. But this is special. Not only is the love of his life, Pam, coming into the house, but so is Troy, carrying something

carefully wrapped in a blanket. He has an idea . . .
to show them *his* blanket! The moment they
come through the door, he runs around excitedly,
dragging the blanket smelling like sweet baby
powder behind.

When Pam shows him the tiny infant wrapped in
a baby blanket—which smells just like his—Bullet
knows he has a new friend. Also, a new job . . . to
watch out for this little creature.

For Pam it was such a relief to be home, sleeping in
her own bed. She smiled and said a little prayer before she
closed her eyes on the image of her two babies: baby Troy
an arm's length away, and Bullet, her baby secret service
agent, taking up his station underneath the bassinet.

Over the next two weeks Bullet sees more activity
in the household than he can ever remember. There
are not only new smells, but noises. He doesn't like
one bit to hear baby Troy crying.

Troy Sr. had taken off three weeks when the baby arrived
on April 10 and wasn't due back to work until May 1. And
there seemed to be more visitors than usual wanting to see
the baby. For each one Bullet had to show off his blanket.

You also never had to ask where the dog was; wherever baby Troy was, so was Bullet.

> He watches Pam feed the little tyke with a bottle. Unfortunately, nothing falls on the floor, so there are no scraps. But Pam takes care of that. She always makes sure he gets a little treat. That's one of the things he loves about her. Always thoughtful.

May 1, 4:30 a.m.

Buzz.

Troy clicked off his alarm clock at 4:30, rolled out of bed, and headed for the shower. He was finally going back to work.

Pam, awakened by the alarm, slid out of bed and took a peek at the baby. In the dim light, he looked fine. She reached out and patted Bullet down below.

As long as she was up, she decided she might as well warm a bottle and feed the baby a little early. Sliding into her slippers, she scuffed down the hall to the kitchen.

> *Woof, woof, woof!*

Bullet's barking, rarely heard, and never at this time of day, alarmed her.

"Bullet! What's the matter?" said Pam, coming into the hallway. Bullet was more animated than he'd been in years, literally jumping on the parquet floor, rushing back and forth, continuing to bark.

Following Bullet, Pam rushed into the bedroom to the bassinet. The baby was motionless. *But is he sleeping?* She reached down, swooped him up, and walked rapidly toward the light near the bathroom. She was horrified by what she saw. The baby looked like he was crying . . . but no sound was coming out! She watched her baby turn from red-faced to purplish blue.

"Troy, Troy!" she screamed, holding the baby against her shoulder, patting his back, entering the bathroom where Troy was wrapped in a towel.

Recognizing the emergency, Troy briskly lifted the baby from Pam, shouting "Call 911!" He quickly carried the baby to the bed, laid him on his side, and patted his back, hoping to dislodge anything that was clogging his throat.

Troy's mind raced to a movie he had seen in high school, about CPR. *What did it say to do?* He held the baby by his ankles, again gently patting his back.

A woman's voice on the speakerphone was now filling the room. Bullet started barking. Pam, in a panicked voice, said, "This is an emergency! My newborn baby is not breathing! Please come quickly!"

The operator asked for her address and calmly instructed Pam to unlock the door so the EMT team could get in, which she did, as she carried the phone with her.

Apparently, the computer screen at the dispatcher's end provided her with added information. She said, surprised, "One EMT is on his way right now! He lives in your neighborhood."

Woof, woof, woof!

Bullet was hearing someone approaching. The EMT bounded through the open door and took the baby from Troy, all the while asking questions to establish what had happened.

"This is unusual," said the 911 operator, still on the phone with Pam. "Another EMT—also from your neighborhood—is coming from ten houses away." Again with a bewildered tone in her voice, she said, "He'll also be there ahead of the ambulance, which is only a few more minutes away."

Woof, woof, woof!

Bullet was at the door again as the second EMT rushed in. Moments later, Bullet announced the arrival of the ambulance team, followed by local police and firemen.

Once the emergency medical technicians had the baby stabilized and breathing again, they advised Pam and Troy which hospital they were proceeding to: Brookhaven Medical Center, only seven minutes away versus a half hour to Stony Brook University Hospital, where the baby had been born. One parent could ride in the ambulance; they suggested it be Troy, who was already dressed, and asked if Pam could meet them there in her own car.

"Yes, yes. Go. I'll follow you," said Pam frantically.

As he quickly packed his gear, the EMT said to Troy, "Another few seconds and I'm afraid we would have lost your baby. Your dog is a hero!"

Pam looked at him blankly with wide eyes. *Thank God for Bullet* . . . but also . . . *I have to get to the hospital!*

5:30 a.m.

As Pam quickly threw on some slacks and a blouse and grabbed her car keys and a light jacket, she thought, *God . . . what if Bullet had not insisted that I go look at the baby at that very minute?*

She kneeled down to hug her rescuer. "I love you, Bullet. My hero."

Looking up, she said, "God, we're still not out of the woods! Please help the doctors find out why my baby stopped breathing!"

Hastily, she said, "Bullet, you be a good boy. We'll . . ." Her voice cracked. ". . . I hope we'll be back soon."

She cried as she ran out the door. About to get into her minivan, she saw a predicament. Troy's Dodge Daytona was blocking her in. There was no way around it, not even driving across the lawn. She turned, dashed back into the house, grabbed the other keys from the rack, and, without pausing, ran to Troy's vehicle, just as she remembered . . . *Oh, no . . . I can't drive this! It's a stick shift. I don't know how.*

For a moment she stood in the driveway, crying, stunned and dumbfounded. But her mission was critical. She had no choice. She climbed into the Dodge—sniffling back tears and breathing heavily—and started the car. She tried to move the shift, pleading with herself to remember. *How did you tell me to do it, Troy?*

"God, I need Your help right now! I don't know how to drive this thing and my baby needs me!" she yelled.

She tried again. Remembered something about a "clutch." She pushed it down with her foot and pulled the gearshift. The vehicle jumped and jerked, but she managed to back into the street, narrowly missing a parked car. She braked in a sudden stop, then repeated, clutching and shifting, this time in forward. The car jerked ahead again, but Pam was a desperate mother trying to get to her baby, frightened and crying all the way to Brookhaven Medical Center. If you had asked her where she parked the Dodge, she couldn't have told you. She just ran as fast as she could into the emergency room, shouting, "I'm here to see my baby!"

Pam embraced Troy, who was in the waiting room. He looked tense, telling Pam he hadn't heard anything yet.

Just then a nurse emerged and said the baby was stabilized and breathing evenly. She said Pam could come with her to see the baby.

Pam remained worried as she saw a young nurse tending to baby Troy. The nurse seemed tentative and inexperienced. She watched as the nurse started to remove the EKG lines from the baby, attached by adhesives. Pam instinctively opened her mouth to shout "No!" just as the young lady began to rip the sticky pads from the baby.

Too late! The ripping sound was followed by the baby's face again contorting into a fierce cry that produced no sounds. Again, the child's face turned from red to purplish blue. Pam didn't know what to do!

"Can anybody do something?" she shouted.

A more experienced nurse, who was supposed to have

left work already, was walking past the door to the room when she heard the commotion. She looked in and knew exactly what to do. She lifted the baby lengthwise, raising it so the child's face was even with her own face; then, like she was playing a flute, she oxygenated the baby by blowing across its nose and mouth.

The baby took a breath!

A doctor—who was also supposed to be off duty, but was still there—rushed into the room and began making arrangements for the child and Pam to be transported to Stony Brook University Hospital, which had a far more sophisticated neonatal clinic, and was more capable of dealing with this emergency.

Again, Pam's heart was racing. Again, she was witnessing the rescuing of her baby. And again, she thanked God for the blessings and Godwinks.

Returning to Stony Brook University Hospital, where Pam had birthed baby Troy, was a comfort for Pam and Troy. She was more confident that Stony Brook had the resources to determine what was wrong.

Over the course of the next two weeks, baby Troy was diagnosed with silent reflux, a backing up of the stomach contents into the baby's underdeveloped esophagus, which was complicated by the discovery of a curvature of the spine.

May 15, 2002—Stony Brook University Hospital

As Troy handled the paperwork for the baby to be released from the hospital, Pam recounted their blessings with Troy's mom, Irene. Their baby was now safe, thanks to a small army of heroes.

"Bullet was the biggest hero of all!" she said excitedly, rattling off the other Godwinks that had flowed from his actions at the start of the crisis. What were the odds that two EMTs lived in the neighborhood and had arrived ahead of the ambulance? And what about the nurse at Brookhaven Medical Center, who was just walking past the doorway at the exact moment she was needed, and who knew how to do CPR on an infant? She was supposed to be off duty; same as the doctor.

Then there were all the other first responders and medical personnel who quietly saved lives every day, but were divinely aligned to be at the right place at the right moment to help save tiny Troy.

Troy then rejoined Pam and his mom. "Honey, when Bullet got my attention that morning, it was a miracle, wasn't it?" observed Pam.

Troy nodded, turning to his mom to share evidence of Bullet's heroism: "The EMT said a few seconds more and we would have lost our baby."

"People need to know about this," said Irene. "We can't keep God's blessing to ourselves. We have to share it."

Troy wasn't sure where she was going with that comment.

Irene already had an idea. When she left the hospital, she called a friend . . . someone who worked for *Newsday*.

May 15, 2002—*Newsday* Offices, Melville, NY

Ann noticed an unusual lightheartedness, more animated voices, as several reporters gathered around the editor's desk.

Alex Martin, the gruff but dedicated and demanding editor of *Newsday*, was holding court, telling about the call he had just received from a woman who said an old dog had saved a newborn baby.

After eight months of the reporters slogging their way through daily stories of horror, and of heroic firemen and police in unthinkable circumstances, here was a simple Norman Rockwell story about a dog that saved the life of a baby in crisis. But it wasn't just any dog—it was a dog who himself had been saved earlier when the parents of the baby, against all reasonable advice, had scraped up the money to perform a $5,000 operation on their fourteen-year-old dog.

This was a story about life . . . and living . . . and it was lifting the hearts of all the reporters who were gathered to hear it.

"Givens, you've got this assignment."

Ann's heart jumped. *What? I'm the one who gets a day pass from news agony in order to bring the public something that will make them smile and warm their hearts?*

"This could be a hoax. Check it out. After you talk to the parents, talk to the EMTs, the police, the firemen who showed up . . . validate everything," said Alex.

Ann nodded, hoping she wasn't inappropriately smiling or looking giddy.

"And get me audio of the dog barking."

Ann looked at her editor questioningly. "Audio?"

"Yes, audio." Then, anticipating the unstated question *Why*, he answered, "Because we're a newspaper in a brand-new world!" Which wasn't all that helpful.

An hour later Ann was pulling into the driveway of Pam and Troy Sica's home in Bellport.

She knocked on the door and Pam answered.

As Pam and Troy relived the story, showing Ann where the baby's bassinet sat next to the bed, where Bullet was on watch, underneath, Ann took copious notes.

At the end of the interview, Ann said, "Ah, do you think we could get Bullet to bark, so I can record it?"

Pam and Troy looked at her blankly.

"I . . . don't know why, actually . . . My editor just asked me to record the dog barking."

> Bullet answers the call to come into the living room, momentarily leaving his guard duty under the bassinet, but he has no idea what they are talking about when they keep saying, "Bark, Bullet, bark!" He politely remains quiet.

Troy then suggested, "How about going outside and ringing the doorbell, pretending to be the mailman. The only time Bullet barks is when the mailman comes!"

It worked.

🐾   🐾   🐾

As Ann drove back to *Newsday*, she calculated that she had about two hours before her deadline to turn in the story to Alex, and she had a good number of calls to make to verify it.

Then she took a moment to just feast on the good feelings running through her—she was tickled pink!

Later, Alex liked the story and said he thought she had done a good job. But the real accolades came the next day.

A rarity since the tragedy of 9/11, *Newsday* had a joyful story on the front page! There was a photo of Bullet nuzzled next to a baby with the headline: "His Best Friend."

The headline above the story inside the paper read: "A LIFE-SAVING BULLET—Family Dog Alerts Mom to Baby in Distress, Just in Time."

Ann was gratified that she had finally written a feel-good story that seemed to bring hope to so many readers.

It was a day or two later before Ann found out what her editor had in mind by having Bullet bark. Internet usage was still new and *Newsday* was working on adding authenticity to their online stories with pieces of audio and video.

Just as Alex had thought, many readers, after reading the story, wanted to hear a word or two, right from the mouth of the hero himself: Bullet's barking.

May 2002—Bellport, Long Island

> After Pam shows him his picture on the cover of
> that newspaper, Bullet notices that people seem to
> be making a big fuss over him. Go figure.

Pam and Troy have never stopped thanking God for the decision they made that day with Dr. Cangro at Bellport Animal Hospital. The $5,000 loan to keep Bullet alive was the best investment of their lives, not to mention Troy Jr.'s life.

The dog they saved, saved their son.

Reflections

Two years later, Pam was again holding her sweet dog in her arms with tears flowing down her cheeks. She was once more looking deeply into Bullet's eyes. He again seemed to be communicating to her in a wordless language . . . this time saying, "I have no more to do . . . I'm ready to go."

At the age of sixteen he closed his eyes, drifting peacefully away.

As of this writing, Troy Jr. has entered college. Pam and Troy are both still working, devoted to each other and their son and their memory of Bullet.

Ann Givens now writes for an online magazine called *The Trace*, while her husband, Rafer, has moved on to his wife's old stomping grounds—*Newsday*. He's the paper's movie reviewer.

As long as we're telling dogwink stories from a reporter's point of view, let's do one more: Keller.

7

KELLER

John Gray, an up-and-coming TV news reporter, placed his fingers on the keys and began typing. The words had rolled through his mind as to how he would present the book to his publisher . . . a children's book about a little girl who couldn't hear, whose parents brought home a deaf and blind dog.

Clicking the keys furiously, he wrote:

The girl is Raven. She's deaf. Children at school are hesitant to play with her, as if she'll break.

The hero is a dog, whose first owner left the puppy, who was deaf and blind, by the side of the road.

At that moment, John's deaf and blind dog, a white Australian shepherd, nudged him.

> Keller senses John is in the chair. He sniffs until he
> finds his hand. He licks it.

"Keller, how you doing, boy? I'm writing a book about you," John said, ruffling the dog's neck. "It's going to tell your story in a different way . . . with a fictional little girl named Raven. You'll love her."

John's mind drifted to that day months earlier when he'd joined a dozen of his Channel 10 colleagues volunteering at an Albany, NY, animal shelter. The shelter manager asked if he could help move some things in a back room. As John hefted several crates onto a table, he came across a cage. Something was in it. A furry, white, frightened little puppy.

"He's deaf and blind," volunteered the manager, shaking her head. "Someone left him beside the road."

"Does that happen often?" John asked.

She nodded slightly. "All too often."

"Can I hold him?" asked John.

As John stroked the pup's soft white fur, the tiny thing seemed to shiver slightly. He covered the little dog with his arms to keep him warm.

The world is dark. And silent. But the pup smells a strong male scent, and feels muscular arms around him. He feels safe. Safer than ever before.

"What's the likelihood that he'll be adopted?" asked John gingerly.

"Slim to none," the manager said sadly.

"I wish I could help this little guy," said John, handing the pup back to the manager, "but I've got three German shepherds at home. I'm afraid of what they'd do to a helpless pup like this."

The little dog is put back in the cage. He whimpers slightly, wishing the strong man would pick him up again.

Over the next two weeks, John couldn't get the little dog out of his mind. He stopped by the animal shelter twice to see if anyone had adopted the deaf and blind puppy.

"No," said the manager, her voice trailing off as she confided that her colleagues had recommended that the little dog be put down.

John told his wife, Courtney, about the pup, repeating his fear that their big dogs might cause harm to a helpless puppy.

Courtney knew her husband. His heart was aching for that little pup. "How will you know unless you try?" she said with a smile.

John just looked at her. If he wasn't mistaken, she had just given him an open door to bring home another pup.

The next day he returned to the animal shelter and arranged to take the little dog home, "Just for a visit," he said to the manager.

> The little dog is excited. He is being held by the man again! Yay! Then he is taking him somewhere.
>   He is riding next to the man and feeling the movements of a car.

Courtney came to the door as John brought the little dog into the house. He placed the tiny creature in the middle of the kitchen floor and carefully watched the reaction of the German shepherds.

The big dogs appeared menacing as they slowly moved toward the little puppy lying motionless on the floor.

> *Uh-oh.* The pup smells other dogs! Very close! It's best to sit still, like in a ball . . . maybe they won't notice him.

They walked around the little dog, sniffing him.

"I am really surprised," John said quietly to Courtney. "I think they know this little dog is special. Look how they're checking him out. Curious, but kind."

"Something tells me we have a new member of the family," said Courtney.

John beamed. He loved that his wife had such a beautiful heart. He looked at her and said, "I think I have the perfect name for him. 'Keller.'" He paused. "As in Helen Keller."

Courtney hugged him. She then reached down and picked up Keller, hugging him as the other dogs looked on.

> Now Keller is liking the scent of the woman who picked him up! Then the man is carrying him in his strong arms. Oh, this feels nice . . . warm water.

John decided to give Keller his first bath in his new home. He pulled out a large basin and filled it with warm water. Keller seemed to like it.

John rubbed what looked like a dirty patch on his white fur. He looked again. It wasn't dirt at all. It was a patch of dark fur, in the shape of a heart. Then, on the bottom of one paw, John spotted the shape of another heart. Little dogwinks from Keller to his new family.

As a reporter, John Gray used writing as a tool for his job, but it was also his hobby and therapy. Whenever he wanted to get his mind off things, he'd sit down and simply pour out thoughts through his fingers on the keys.

That's how he came up with the notion to write a children's book, inspired by Keller.

John studied how the pup developed a superior capability with his senses of smell, touch, and taste, offsetting his inability to hear and see. By smell and touch, Keller learned to map out the house and find his way around. Sometimes, just touching his tongue to something would help him identify things.

John wove these real-life observations about Keller into the children's book with the fictional little girl, Raven. Together they demonstrated that the differences we are born with can be tools for inclusion. He wrote:

Even though Raven was deaf she did all the things other children did at school. She taught them simple sign language like "hello" and "how are you?"

As the other children looked on, Raven took a bowl of water and put it on the floor with the puppy. She took his paw and tapped it twice. Then allowed him a sip.

"What's Raven doing?" asked one of the children.

The teacher smiled and said, "Teaching him doggie sign language."

A few months later John opened a package that came in the mail. He let Keller smell it.

> Keller sniffs. A different smell. Like paper. Then he
> licks it. That is different too. The faint taste of glue.
> Wonder what it is?

"Keller . . . this book is all about you," John said, petting the pup. "I wish you could see it. There's a drawing of you on the cover and it shows the little heart in your fur. And what do we call this book? *Keller's Heart.* You're going to be famous."

John had no idea how much.

When a big bookstore in Albany promoted a book signing with the opportunity to meet Keller in person, everyone was astonished with the outcome.

The line of people outside the bookstore waiting to get in to meet Keller stretched around the block. More than eight hundred people!

> Keller can smell all sorts of different perfumes and
> recognizes the smell of children. He likes those the

best. Then he can feel different hands caressing
him . . . big hands and small hands.
   He likes them all!

John subsequently discovered that Keller was an ambassador of hope for children in hospitals and nursing-home patients. Just as he'd written in the book: "For a dog trapped in darkness, Keller was full of light."

One day John was telling someone how lucky he was that day when the animal shelter manager had asked him to help move some crates in the back room. The person had a different perspective: "Maybe that wasn't luck at all, but a Godwink!"

Indeed.

Reflections

The sweet deaf and blind dog, once left by the side of the road like a bag of trash, is today a celebrity dog touching the hearts of thousands. Even more important, Keller is a canine ambassador for God, delivering hope and encouragement to people young and old, in schools and hospitals.

We are ambassadors for Christ,
since God is making his appeal through us.
—2 CORINTHIANS 5:20*

Keller's birthday is February 14—Valentine's Day. Isn't that appropriate for this dog of many hearts?

---

* New American Standard Bible.

8

SAMMY

He was the size of a large cat. A cute, skinny Westie.

Everyone in the East 79th Street apartment building would see Sammy excitedly tugging on his leash, so glad to be taking his morning run with his owner.

Oh boy, thinks Sammy, starting his daily routine of "hellos" to everyone he encounters, like a little politician.

He dances a little jig as Mrs. Spitzer the neighbor opens her door to pick up the morning paper; excitedly licks the hand of Walter the elevator man; zigzags among the shoes of nearly everyone waiting in the lobby; offers a special daily greeting to Carlos the doorman, the keeper of the doggie treats.

Sammy's first name was pronounced, as you might expect, "Sammy."

His owner Richard Tempchine's first name was pronounced "REE-shar." He was French—a producer of independent films. Richard's lyrical, French-accented "Good morning" was almost as welcoming as seeing Sammy trying to pull this grown man out onto the sidewalk, faster than he wanted to go.

As was the case every day, Sammy went jogging in Central Park with Richard. They would run quite some distance from home, as far as thirty blocks north to 109th Street. Sammy always stayed very close to Richard, particularly in strange places.

In return for this good behavior, Richard would unhook Sammy's leash.

Ahhh . . . that is always a treat for Sammy. The freedom to scamper a little! Not too far. He stays very close to Richard.

If dogs could whistle, that's what Sammy would be doing. Zip-a-dee-doo-dah. Expressing joy to everyone he encounters.

GRRRR . . . GRRRROWL!

Sammy jumps a foot in the air. YIKES!

It is the world's biggest Doberman, teeth bared, leaping from the shadows, snarling, inches from Sammy's face!

Sammy bolts. He has to get away!

Like the Gingerbread Man, *run, run, run as fast as you can!*

Richard heard the commotion of the big dog and looked down to assure himself that Sammy was right there beside him. He wasn't! What? He stopped. Looked in every direction. There were dozens of people on the sidewalk obstructing his view. *Oh no . . . which way did he go?*

The Doberman was yanking on the chain around his neck, which was attached to a fence, as his owner was now trying to calm him.

Sammy runs like the wind until he realizes the Doberman isn't on his tail anymore; it's safe to slow down.

He has no idea where he is. As a city dog, he only goes to places close to Richard's 79th Street apartment or the regular route in and out of Central Park. And always—except when they are jogging—on his owner's leash.

Richard was heartsick. He looked everywhere. He dreaded going home and facing Jill, his wife, with the terrible news that Sammy was lost. Worse was the prospect of telling their nine-year-old daughter, Chloe, when she returned from school.

"But he has a name tag," said Jill in a voice choked with emotion, after learning the news. "Perhaps somebody will find him and call us."

Richard shrugged. The prospect of someone stopping and looking at Sammy's collar seemed unlikely at that moment.

But he had to take action. He enlisted friends and laid out assignments for each person to search a specific quadrant of Central Park. They would rendezvous back at the apartment, hopefully with good news, before Chloe got home at 3:00 p.m.

The searchers spread out. They looked and looked. Up one pathway of the park and down another, calling out "Sammy, Sammy!"

By 2:45 p.m. the searchers reassembled at the apartment, each bearing a dejected countenance and with nothing to report.

Sammy is wandering aimlessly through Central Park. It is vast. In human terms, two-and-a-half miles long and a half-mile across. He is hopelessly lost.

Then his ears perk up. He hears the familiar squeaking and engine noises of a city bus stopping. Then the whooshing sound as the stairs lower

to allow passengers to board. He runs toward
familiarity.

As he emerges from the park, the adjacent street
is busy with traffic, cars, buses, and yellow cabs,
each jockeying to move along. The air is filled with
honking sounds.

He joins some people crossing the street at a light,
and spots a doorman holding a hose, washing down
the sidewalk in front of a New York building.

Ahhh . . . a few licks of refreshment from the little
puddle on the sidewalk.

What's that? A voice . . . speaking in a foreign
language . . . again, something that was familiar and
comforting . . . *Let's see who that is.*

The housekeeper had left a note. Someone had called
about Sammy.

Richard dialed the number.

"*Bonjour* . . ." answered a voice on the other end of the
line.

"I'm sorry, I must have the wrong number," said Richard in his heavily accented English, thinking he must
have dialed a French establishment by mistake. He dialed
again.

"*Bonjour* . . ." answered the voice again.

"Hello," said Richard, hesitantly. "Someone left this number to call . . . about my missing dog. My name is Richard Tempchine."

"*Oui, monsieur*," said the lady, in a French accent even thicker than Richard's, "this is the French Embassy on Fifth Avenue. Your little puppy has come to visit us. He is in our garden, right now. And we noticed a tag with your number."

A burst of joy!

Somehow little Sammy had traveled thirty New York City blocks and arrived at a place he'd never visited before—the French Embassy!

As Chloe got off the bus at 79th Street, her dad was there to greet her. And to tell her that they were going to take a walk down 5th Avenue, to the French Embassy. On the way, he told her about the great Godwink. A bilingual dogwink!

Reflections

Being lost is a terrible feeling—for those who are lost and for those who are trying to find them.

Were you ever in a situation like this? Your three- or four-year-old is right by your side in a department store. A clerk asks if you need help. Your attention is momentarily diverted. In that split second your child is suddenly out of sight among dozens of ladies' dress racks. From where you stand it's impossible to see where your little tyke has gone. A wave of panic rushes into your chest. You cry out as you race around, shouting to others to help you find your child!

While we may not know exactly the fear little Sammy had that day he was lost in Central Park, we can empathize, to some degree, with the anxiety that Richard and his wife were feeling.

Of course, the best lost-and-found department is God's. The first line of defense is to pray. And when that prayer is answered, it frequently is in the form of a Godwink.

9

OZZIE

Some people would call Ozzie a "Minnie Jack," which is a cross between a Jack Russell terrier and a miniature Doberman pinscher. He was just fine being known as "Ozzie."

The small black-and-brown pup didn't know it, but he was named after someone important: Chicago White Sox coach Ozzie Guillen. That's because his owners, Eric and Amy, were such big baseball fans. Come to think of it, the two Ozzies had something in common: they both loved to play catch!

Minnie Jacks are energetic dogs. They can jump about four feet in the air and they love humans.

Ozzie was particularly fond of Eric's mom, Brenda Larson. She called him her little "lover boy."

During the summer, Brenda was visiting Eric and Amy

at their home in Illinois. Ozzie spent a lot of time with Brenda during the day, so at nighttime, Amy put up a gate at the entrance to their bedroom to keep her friendly little dog from wandering off.

It was a sweltering night. Brenda hadn't been feeling well and she awoke at 2:30 in the morning, making her way to the bathroom. Suddenly she felt a loss of control! The room was spinning. She collapsed on the bathroom floor with her legs extending into the hallway.

Ozzie, not a barking dog, looks through the gate and sees that Brenda is in trouble! He bolts back, jumps up on the bed, begins bouncing, then— uncharacteristically—barking.

"Ozzie! What's the matter?" said Amy, startled.

The pup leaps to the floor and runs to the gate. He dashes back and forth, barking until Amy gets up and follows him.

Amy saw Brenda and rushed to check on her.

Brenda remembers coming to, with Amy shaking her, and Ozzie snuggled next to her, pressing his face to hers.

Amy was authoritative. "Brenda, we're calling 911!"

"No, no, I'm all right," said Brenda weakly, trying to sound stronger than she was.

Amy wouldn't hear of it, and dialed the number. Soon sirens were heard in the distance.

> Ozzie hangs close to Brenda, never leaving her side,
> right up until the paramedics arrive and rush her to
> the hospital.

Doctors discovered that Brenda had a major bleeding ulcer requiring four units of blood. Later, her doctor looked at her solemnly, saying, "I heard what happened. You can thank Ozzie for saving your life. A few minutes more and you wouldn't have made it."

From that day forward, Brenda has referred to Ozzie— to anyone and everyone—as "my hero." In appreciation for his heroism, she bought him a designer-label collar made of brown leather and gold.

As Amy placed it on Ozzie, she said, "This is very expensive, Ozzie."

> Ozzie has no idea what that means, but he really
> likes the collar because it is a gift from Brenda.
> After all, he is her "lover boy."

Reflections

After an experience like Brenda's, it's natural to start making a list of the "what-ifs."

What if she had been home alone when she passed out due to the bleeding ulcer, not visiting her son's family—and Ozzie?

What if Ozzie was the kind of dog that wasn't sensitive to someone being in trouble and failed to alert Eric and Amy?

It does make you stop and think. Only God can reach through the veil between heaven and earth and make His presence known through a very special Godwink.

10

SASHA

Is a dog inherently capable of discerning, even as a puppy, the vulnerable nature of a human infant? Somewhere deep inside, is the puppy drawn as a protector to that child? Perhaps Sasha's story provides a clue.

🐾　🐾　🐾

"Sasha, stop it!" laughed Nana Chaichanhda as her seven-month-old dark-gray pit bull tried to lick the face and arms of her eight-month-old baby. Nana was changing the baby on the bed, getting her into a onesie for the night.

> Sasha loves that sweet-smelling child. She always
> wants to be right near baby Masailah. But then . . .
> who could resist kissing that soft baby skin?

Sasha feels herself being gently pushed away as
Nana finishes dressing the baby.

Oh well, I have to go out anyways, thinks the pup,
jumping from the bed, heading for the back door.

Nana knew the routine. She picked up Masailah and
followed Sasha, opening the door to the enclosed yard behind the four-unit apartment building in Stockton, California.

"Go ahead, Sasha," said Nana.

Nana returned to her bedroom at the front of the
building and placed the baby next to her on the bed as she
clicked on the eleven o'clock news. A single mom, she was
enjoying the unusual quiet of the evening. Her two older
kids, eight and nine, were having an overnight at their
grandmother's.

Sasha romps through the yard. *Wheeee.* She comes
to a sudden halt and takes care of the call of nature.
Then bounds off again, enjoying the feel of her long
ears flapping in the fresh air on this pleasant June
evening.

The pup feels safe in the small backyard. And it is
fun to let out energy chasing fireflies and other tiny
creatures of the night.

Sasha knows that whenever she wants to go
back inside, she just needs to scratch on the
screen door.

But, on a night like this, why hurry?

I'll just take a snooze here on the grass.

An hour later, the baby was sleeping, the program Nana
was watching was finishing, and it crossed her mind that
Sasha had been out longer than usual. But . . . it was nice
out, and the yard was safe, so she didn't worry.

Sasha's nap in the yard is abruptly interrupted. First,
she smells it. *Pew. What's that?*

Then she sees it . . . billowing up from the
neighboring apartment. Smoke!

The pup runs to the door! This is an emergency!
She slams her small body against the screen door . . .
over and over again . . . barking . . . trying to get
Nana's attention immediately!

Nana was confused. Why was Sasha making such a
commotion? She'd never done that before.

Nana was puzzled when she opened the door and the
pup ran right past her down the hall. She quickly followed. Entering the bedroom, her eyes widened and her

jaw dropped. Sasha was on the bed, tugging the baby by her onesie toward the edge!

"Sasha, what are you doing?"

Nana rushed over, grabbed the baby just in time . . . but then . . . she could smell the smoke herself!

With the baby under her arm, she grabbed her phone and bolted for the front door.

"C'mon, Sasha!" she ordered.

Now she could see it! The front of her neighbor's unit was totally engulfed in flames.

With her free hand she dialed 911.

Minutes later, fire engines filled the street as the flames threatened the entire structure, including Sasha's home. She was heartsick. But so grateful at the same time.

She looked at her puppy. Then at her baby. She knew in her heart that Sasha's presence in her life was meant to be.

Her mind flashed to four months earlier when her cousin had unexpectedly showed up with Sasha, saying she'd brought her a gift.

A gift? she recalls thinking at the time. *I don't think I can possibly handle a new dog* and *a new baby.*

Now, beyond all doubt, Sasha the pup had proven her purpose. She *was* a gift . . . a dogwink hero.

Reflections

Godwinks show up unexpectedly in your life, just when you need them.

It's as if God comes along and leaves a beautiful gift on your doorstep.

It's up to us to open the door—to Him—and discover our gift.

TRIXIE

The trim young soldier, eighteen-year-old Bill Morris, hefted the heavy duffel bag packed with all his gear as he stepped down the gangplank.

He looked out across a vast sea of soldiers, ten thousand or more, gathered on a gray dock, against gray skies, among buildings that had been decimated by enemy bombs. Southampton, England, was Bill's first time traveling outside the United States in his life. A new feeling arose within him. Was it fear? Or was it just . . . uncertainty?

> The little tan terrier dashes past the legs of more people than she's ever seen. The pup hops over duffel bags on the dock, zigs and zags, not sure where her internal compass is taking her.

Then she stops. Her eyes lock upon a kind-faced
young man coming off the big ship.

Maybe he's the one!

In some ways, Bill was invigorated to finally be going to
war after three years of training. Scary, for sure, but this was
the patriotic call he'd felt that day he'd sneaked off Staten
Island, taken the ferry, and signed up for the US Army's
Harlem Hellfighters.

Now, everything was different. England was a nation relentlessly pummeled by German air attacks, leaving a sharp,
post-bombing odor in the air, mixed with the strident smell
of axle grease. It was the feeling of being close to war.

He said a silent prayer. *Please, God, let me come home
safe. And please . . . don't let me be captured and put into one
of those prisoner-of-war camps.* Suddenly a feeling of reassur-
ance flashed over him—like a prayer instantly answered—
as he locked eyes with a furry little tan creature. The dog
was staring back at him.

Woof, woof.

She wags her tail, standing as tall as she can among
all the soldiers.

Woof, woof. Over here. Waiting for you!

Bill stepped into the huge crowd of soldiers and, as quickly as she'd appeared, the pup was gone. He looked this way and that. Maybe it ran off.

Then he felt something hit his boot. The little pup was standing right next to him and had dropped a stone on his foot.

He laughed, leaned down, and stroked the wiry fur of the terrier. A female.

"Hi, there. Are you my greeter? Who do you belong to?" he said, looking around for anyone who looked like the owner. No one did.

Bill's attention was snapped back to his mission—he had to stay with his all-black unit of 150 sergeants, the 369th Harlem Hellfighters, now part of the 4251st Quartermaster Truck Company. He stood and caught sight of others from his group starting to move away, toward jeeps and trucks that were being loaded. He walked off, leaving the dog behind.

"I'm riding with you, Sarge," said the friendly corporal, pointing to the nearby jeep.

Bill smiled. He liked Corporal Johnson. He was older, with an aura of strength yet kindness, like Bill's dad. During their prior assignments, the two had never gotten to know each other all that well, but there was an ease between them. Now, both were noncommissioned officers, with Bill holding the higher rank.

Bill slipped behind the wheel.

"You like driving?" asked the corporal.

"Yes. Love it," Bill said with a smile. "When I was six or seven, my dad would sit me on his lap and let me steer the trucks around the property of our family business. We have a moving company back on Staten Island. By the time I was a teen, Dad taught me how to drive those tractor trailers on my own. He'd brag that his son could back a moving truck into a tight spot as well as any of his professional drivers.

"I'm not sure my dad wasn't exaggerating a tiny bit," he said, holding up his thumb and forefinger almost touching, "but driving this jeep should be a snap."

The two men laughed.

🐾 🐾 🐾

In the military you learn to wait. Then, out of the blue, you get an order that requires instant action. "Atte-e-e-n-tion! Convoy, move out!" was the command that came over the bullhorn. Slowly Bill began to drive into alignment with other vehicles.

Woof, woof!

The little terrier has been following the scent of

the man others called "Sarge" or "Bill." Now the
pup sees the vehicle he is in. It's driving away!

Woof, woof.

Corporal Johnson looked down at the little dog running
alongside the still slow-moving jeep.

"Looks likes you have another passenger who wants to
get on board," he said jovially.

"It's that little terrier that came up to me when I got off
the ship," said Bill.

"She wants to go with us, Sarge," said the corporal,
looking at Bill. Then, looking down, "C'mon, girl."

Instantly the pup jumps into the jeep, barking, as if to
say, *Let's go, guys.*

She takes a spot in between the two front seats of
the jeep and is rewarded as both men start to pet her.

"Looks like we got a new recruit." Corporal Johnson
smiled.

"I wonder if she has a name," mused Bill. "Are you . . .
ah . . . Lady?"

"Duchess?" offered the corporal.

"How 'bout Trixie?" asked Bill.

Woof. Woof.

Trixie. That sounds like a nice name.

Corporal Johnson rocked back and forth, laughing. "She likes it!"

"You have a name!" said Bill. "Trixie."

During the nearly two-hour convoy drive to the staging area, Bill and Corporal Johnson chatted amiably. The corporal continued to remind Bill of his dad, always asking questions, showing he was interested in people.

"You married, Sarge?"

Bill nodded. And grinned. "I married my childhood sweetheart on a two-day pass, five hours before we shipped out."

"No kiddin'. Tell me about her," said Corporal Johnson.

"Well, Norcie is really pretty and really sweet." He smiled as he thought of her. "After my dad taught me how to drive moving trucks, on Sunday afternoons I'd take Norcie for rides around the parking lot. She loved it." He chuckled. "I'd look at her sitting next to me, and her smile was just beautiful. Her bright brown eyes lit up her face. And when we stood at the altar and said our vows, she still had that same smile."

"I'm sure you miss her, Sarge."

A catch was forming in Bill's throat. "Yes. Yes, I do."

Trixie, right on cue, senses the sadness Bill is trying
to hide.

The little pup rests her head on Bill's lap. And, just
as she hoped, he strokes her.

For several subsequent weeks, Bill and his unit remained at the staging area near the English Channel. They
knew there was an impending battle, something big, hap-
pening soon, but for security purposes, information was
very tight.

They knew that large numbers of American and Canadian forces were joining the British armies in the war
against the Germans. They heard scuttlebutt that the Germans were dug in on the other side of the English Channel,
in Northern France, anticipating an invasion by the Allied
forces. But who knew for sure what was truth and what was
just chatter?

On many days, Bill and the sixteen trucks under his
command would be ordered to go on military exercises.
They drove their trucks all day in mud and sand; up steep
inclines, over rocks, dodging boulders, and across a small
lake until water was over the hood.

When they weren't training, they were covering the
undercarriages of the vehicles with grease like they'd been
taught back in the States.

One day early in June they were told to get some rest. All day long, from far away, they could hear the thundering sounds of battle. Then, well before dawn the next morning, they were ordered to pull out. They were to be the second wave in the battle.

Bill and the trucks under his command, carrying supplies for the troops, drove over the sand beach in southwest England and were directed to drive onto open-top vessels. Some fifty LCTs, they called them—Landing Craft Tanks—were lined up, side by side, at the water's edge.

The LCT had a huge door that folded down, allowing four trucks to drive onto the boat. Then it would close up. Bill knew that when they arrived at their destination, the door would fold down into the water and the trucks, tanks, or troops would disembark, driving through the water to the beach.

Sitting right next to him in the front passenger seat was Trixie. Ready for whatever was coming.

Trixie has gotten used to hearing the sounds of war. England has been under siege for months. She's not scared, but she likes sticking close to Bill nonetheless. He protects her. Makes sure she is fed and safe.

He's attached something to her that he calls a

harness. It is tied to a length of rope. Bill holds on to
the other end. She likes knowing that.

Sitting behind the wheel of the truck for what seemed
like three or four hours as they crossed the English Channel, Bill prayed many times. Yet, he was feeling calmer than
he would have expected just before entering the first battle
of his life.

He looked down at Trixie, resting her head on his lap.
The pup did that for me, he thought. When she looked at
him, there was no fear in her eyes. No doubt about it. She
calmed him.

Bill forced his mind to think about good things. He
pictured the gleaming sweet smile of Norcie, the love of
his life. He could then visualize her going to her job as a
nurse, probably getting whistled at by soldiers or construction workers. She was a looker.

Bill's heartstrings were strummed as he imagined her sitting around the table with his family for Sunday dinner, the
most important family gathering of the week. He pictured
his dad asking how his son was doing, knowing that Norcie
would get many more letters than they, his parents, would.

Uh-oh, that makes me feel a little guilty, he thought, forcing his mind back to the present, suddenly noticing that
the thundering sounds of a raging battle were getting closer
and closer. Soon bullets could be heard bouncing off the

sides of the LCT as they approached Omaha Beach. Although the sun was up, the sky was dark with smoke.

"Okay, Trixie, get ready for action," Bill said in a tight voice to his little companion.

He could hear and feel the front side of the LCT lowering. Now his truck . . . the first one in line . . . was exposed to the machine guns' bullets. They were pinging off the truck and the insides of the LCT. He started the engine and drove forward, right into the whizzing bullets.

> Trixie tenses up. The sounds of the battle being
> so close and the movement of the LCT signal that
> something is happening. She can smell smoke in
> the air.
>
> Now she feels the cold water. It is pouring into
> the open sides of the truck. She is floating! Bill is
> concentrating on driving the vehicle.
>
> Things are floating by in the water. Soldiers.
> She can smell fear. And death.
>
> She can hear Bill saying a prayer.

Bill gazed ahead, his hands sweating as he gripped the wheel, trying to control the direction of the truck. He was in deeper water than he'd expected. The strong currents struggled to push him out of control.

The noise was deafening. The smell was awful. But the sight was horrifying. He could see the color of the water. It was red.

Oh God, please protect me. And Trixie. And my unit.

Trixie is suddenly underwater! The currents have dragged her through the open window. She struggles to swim upward. But which direction is up?

Suddenly her body is being yanked. Then, once again, she is back in the truck. Bill used one hand to pull on the rope, while his other steered the truck through a hail of bullets.

He could feel it. Just like they had trained in the lake. The wheels finally grabbed hold of the bottom of the English Channel as he began to drive onto Omaha Beach. He kept powering ahead. Right into the firestorm of bullets. He drove over the sand as quickly as the truck would go, careful not to strike any of his fellow troops, some of whom jumped up and followed, using the truck as a shield.

He wanted to stop and help soldiers in need. But he had orders. *Do not stop. Your job is to get this truck to the top of the cliffs.*

Bill could now see the cliffs, nearly 100 feet high, through the smoke of war. The enemy firepower was raining down on them from above. But if he could make his way to the bottom of the cliff—the seawall—he'd have more protection as he looked for the pathway to the top.

As he drove, he saw dead and wounded . . . white soldiers and black . . . unified by the color of their blood and their love of their country.

Reaching the bottom of the cliff, he drove along, hoping against hope he'd find the way to the top. He also knew there were trucks behind him, counting on his leadership.

Then he saw it—a very precarious route came into view through the smoke. As he started upward, he saw rocks rolling back down at him. He stopped. They just missed him! Then he resumed his ascent. Explosions going off on either side of his truck indicated that the enemy was trying to stop him.

The truck's engine ground and whined but eventually emerged at the top. Friendly troops were already there, directing him where to drive to unload the supplies in territory that had just been captured by the Allied forces.

One by one, other trucks in Bill's unit began to arrive. All sixteen had made it safely to the top. His entire unit.

Trixie is excited to see some of the other drivers, all of whom come by and ruffle her fur. But she is particularly happy to see Corporal Johnson.

Bill was keeping his cool. He wanted to hug and shake hands with his men, but this wasn't the time or place. The sounds of war were only a mile or so away. But he did allow himself a smile when the door opened to one of the trucks and Corporal Johnson climbed down from the driver's seat. At the last minute he had been assigned to take over and drive one of the trucks.

Everyone remarked that it was a miracle that they had all made it. They all thanked God.

Only later would they learn what they'd been through. They were among 156,000 Allied soldiers—Americans, British, and Canadian—who had taken part in the largest invasion in history. The troops stormed five beaches of Normandy in Northern France—Omaha Beach being the fiercest battle. The event would forever be commemorated as D-Day, a day over four thousand soldiers lost their lives. A day that was hailed as the turning point of World War II.

> Trixie looks up at Bill. She is hungry. She hears him say, "Just hold on a bit longer, girl, and I'll feed you, okay?"
>
> She wags her tail. *I'm good,* she wants him to know.

It was about 4 p.m. After nearly two days with no sleep or food, Bill's unit wasn't sure what to do first . . . collapse or eat. They ate. While they finished their C-rations, Bill told them that Trixie and he were going to get their orders.

When he returned, he told the men that they would unload their cargo for the soldiers still fighting on the beaches and then drive to a depot twenty-five or thirty miles away. There, all the trucks would load up supplies that needed to be transported to General Patton's tank corps.

It was a tough grind, but his men put smiles on their faces and said, "Well, here we go again." They were a great bunch.

Bill grabbed some C-rations for himself and opened a can for Trixie. She gobbled it down so fast, he gave her another one.

> Trixie is feeling ready to go back to work. She runs
> to the truck and waits for Bill to help her get up into
> the front seat.

Bill leaned down and said, "Let's go, Trixie," before lifting her up and placing her in between the two front seats as Corporal Johnson climbed into the passenger seat, now reassigned as Bill's sidekick.

As Bill pulled out, he looked into the sideview mirror to see that all the other fifteen trucks were behind him. They all fell into line.

"We'll need to keep a watchful eye," cautioned Corporal Johnson. "There's no way to know when we're behind enemy lines."

Bill's unit was part of the Red Ball Express. As Patton's tanks advanced on the enemy, he constantly needed supplies—fuel, food, water, engine parts, ammo—and Bill and his men were part of the supply chain.

It was hard to keep up with Patton, though. The general's trademark was to move fast and keep the enemy off-balance. Bill's group had to chase General Patton without the benefit of maps or radios. Instead they followed road markers—red circles the size of tennis balls—painted on walls, trees, rocks to point the way to the supply depots. If they didn't see a red ball for a while, they'd have to guess their way there and back.

Sometimes riding over dirt roads is very bumpy. Trixie can find herself flying, all four legs up in the air.

Yet, she is a true soldier. She's not fazed by surprises. She doesn't flinch at the sudden sound of explosions or gunfire around her.

Part of her job is to let Bill know that she has his back. Sometimes she conveys that with just a lick of his hand.

Bill was astonished with Trixie's perceptions. Just when he was feeling a little uncertain or apprehensive, she'd calm him.

They drove and drove into the dark. When they got to where they expected to meet up with General Patton, he was already gone. Even with low supplies he kept on moving.

Once they finally arrived at Patton's encampment and unloaded the trucks, they had only a few hours of sleep before daybreak. They had to circle back to where they came from . . . or where the supply depot had been moved to . . . but rarely did they go back with empty trucks. They were filled with German prisoners of war to take back to a camp stockade.

He knew it was tough for the prisoners he was transporting. But he also knew the treatment they got from Americans was far more humane than that which American POWs received from the Nazis.

The thought served as a reminder: every time he loaded the prisoners into the back, he said the same prayer. *Please, God, keep me safe. And don't let me become a POW.*

Trixie has her sixth sense.

There he goes, praying again, she thinks as she rubs up next to Bill.

For months after D-Day, all through the summer and into the fall, Bill rarely had a night's sleep without tossing and turning, reliving the theater of death that day on Omaha Beach.

Whenever he awoke, he could hear anguished sounds coming from other soldiers asleep on other cots in the dark. Those horrific images were tattooed on everyone's memories . . . impossible to erase . . . yet no one talked about them. Each would carry them in their heads, hearts, and souls until their dying day. They didn't have to talk about what they'd seen; they all knew it.

> Trixie is a soldier of hope for all soldiers. Bill is her main love, but she shares her ability to calm people, as many as she can. In a way, she is her own canine ministry of comfort every day of the war.

🐾 🐾 🐾

It started out as a bright sunny day. Bill had overseen the loading of the trucks for the daily run. Just as he, Corporal Johnson, and Trixie were about to pull out, leading the supply line convoy, a jeep pulled up alongside with three white officers.

The captain said, "Sergeant, drive your truck to the rear of the convoy. I'm taking the lead."

Bill was in shock. "Who are you? You're not taking my convoy," he blurted without thinking who he was talking to.

"I'm your commanding officer."

"Sorry, sir. But . . . do you know where to go?"

"Don't question me, soldier. Do what you're told."

Bill glanced at Corporal Johnson as he pulled the truck out of line and joined at the end.

"He'll be lost in fifteen minutes," said the corporal, under his breath.

Sure enough, within a quarter of an hour the captain had led them past the same tree four times, going in circles.

Then a few miles down the road they came under fire. That was not unusual; in fact, it happened on nearly every run. Bill just knew to keep on driving and not even bother firing back.

Then suddenly the convoy stopped. A driver from the front had been sent back with a message. He said, "The captain wants you to come back to the front of the convoy now. He says you can lead."

Bill and Corporal Johnson said nothing. But they each knew the other was stifling a snicker.

Trixie can read the change in the attitudes of the
two men on either side of her. She wags her tail
to join in the high spirits.

Bill led the convoy to the depot and the trucks unloaded
their supplies.

With disdain in his voice, the white captain looked over
the all-black group and ordered the convoy to return. Perhaps he didn't know, or didn't remember, that they were
supposed to transport prisoners of war on their return trip,
but he was sending the trucks back empty.

Then, turning to Bill and Corporal Johnson, the captain
said, "I have a different assignment for you two." It quickly
became clear that the captain had concluded that he'd been
made to look foolish. And, in his view, Bill and the corporal
were the ones responsible.

"Sergeant, I have a mission for you and the corporal.
Just you two. I want you to pick up a package." He told
them they'd find it at a terminal in a neighboring encampment.

As Bill pulled the truck out and drove past his men
standing at their trucks, they all saluted. They knew exactly
what was going on. It was a setup. A crazy suicide mission
prompted by racial prejudice.

Trixie quietly looks from one man to the other.
Bill and the corporal are silent. But they are
also tense, as if they are ready for something
bad to happen.

Later on, they made it to the terminal. Not surprisingly, there was no package for them to pick up. And no one had ever heard of the captain.

It was getting late as they started back—impossible to make out the red balls on trees and rocks. Soon it was dark altogether. They had no idea where they were. Worse, they had no idea where enemy troops were. They came to a field surrounded by trees. There was a little moonlight. Bill and the corporal decided to take their guns and helmets and crawl under the truck to get some sleep.

Trixie snuggles up to Bill. His body keeps her warmer.
She can tell he's not in a deep sleep. Neither is she.
Trixie first hears the crack of a branch. Then she
smells strangers.
She can hear them walking cautiously toward the
truck!
A low growl right next to Bill's ear alerts him.

Bill jerked awake. He patted Trixie as if to say "Thank you," and looked out from under the truck to see an ominous sight: by the faint light of the moon, he could see the black boots of three Germans creeping toward the vehicle. Bill nudged Corporal Johnson.

Both men felt their bodies tense as they pulled their rifles closer. As the Germans cautiously approached the front of the truck, yanking open a door to look inside, Bill signaled the corporal; they would crawl out from the other side of the truck. Trixie followed.

Bill's heart was pounding as he slowly stood up and heard the Germans talking among themselves on the other side of the truck. He signaled, *You take the one on the right . . . I'll take the left.* They moved around the truck and opened fire.

The soldiers on the left and right went down, giving the soldier in the middle time to lift his weapon to shoot. Trixie was already on her way, sailing up, biting the enemy soldier's arm. His gun went flying just as Bill and the corporal both shot him.

> In the face of danger, Trixie never flinched. She acted. Just like a soldier. That's what Bill tells her later, sounding proud of her.

During basic training, Bill and Corporal Johnson had it drilled into them: when you come into surprise contact with the enemy, never stop and ask yourself, *Is he going to shoot?* That moment of delay will most likely be the last breath you take.

They were soldiers in the nasty business of war. They had carried out their duty. But now it was clear . . . they probably *were* behind enemy lines, and there might be other troops nearby who heard the shots. They needed to get out of there!

Fortunately, the first light of day was just starting to break and hopefully they could find red-ball markers to lead them safely back to camp.

They drove and drove, mile after mile. Not a red ball in sight. They began to worry. Were they driving in circles again . . . heading right back to where they had encountered the enemy?

Corporal Johnson suddenly shouted, "There it is. Up there. On that tree!"

That spray-painted ball never looked so good.

"Good catch, Corporal. We can breathe easier."

🐾 🐾 🐾

Hours later Bill pulled the lumbering army truck into the encampment, smiling to himself as he saw his other drivers breaking into grins as they spotted them. As Bill and Corporal Johnson climbed down from the truck, they heard shouts of joy as fellow soldiers surrounded them, slapping their backs and laughing. It seemed pretty clear that they weren't expecting them back alive.

> Trixie is tickled to see her other friends. And they sure seem glad to see her. Every soldier wants to pat her and ruffle her fur.

Bill reported in to the first sergeant, who looked pleased. "It's good to see you, Sarge," he said, adding in a lower voice, "Not so sure the captain will feel the same."

"With your permission, I'd like to report my return to the captain myself," said Bill, looking at the first sergeant knowingly.

"Permission granted." The first sergeant nodded.

Bill walked to the headquarters tent and approached the captain sitting at a desk.

"We're back, sir. There was no package. But mission accomplished."

The captain stared at Bill with a look of shock on his face, which was turning red with rage. He was speechless.

"Permission to leave, sir?"

The captain, still befuddled for a beat or two, finally nodded as he watched the back of Bill walking tall from the tent.

Bill and the corporal decided not to report their en-

counter with the enemy—the danger they had been in—
nor that Trixie was a hero.

However, a year or so later, the regimental commander
learned of Trixie's heroic act and awarded her a citation.

In his letters home to Norcie, Bill never mentioned the
close call with the enemy—no need to worry her any more
than she already was. But he often wrote about Trixie and
how she was such a bearer of comfort, not only for him,
but all the other soldiers. In fact, many soldiers wrote home
about the tough little terrier that accompanied them onto
fields of battle and always made them feel better.

Bill couldn't wait to receive letters from his pretty wife.
He'd read them over and over, almost memorizing them.
She'd write about the family, who was having a baby, who
got a new job, and so on. Norcie would describe Sunday
dinner at his mom and dad's home, sharing occasional tid-
bits about his ten brothers and sisters or her eight siblings.
She knew he was always interested in the family business,
how the Morris Moving Company was doing.

Norcie would hide a line or two in the letter that only he
should read. Something very sweet and personal. He'd hold
those letters up to his face, smelling the drop of Evening in
Paris perfume that she'd dab onto them just before sealing
the letter with her own lipstick kiss.

At night he'd dream about when he could go home, hug

Norcie, go back to work driving trucks with his dad, and raise a family.

🐾   🐾   🐾

Bill was just waking up when he heard it. An ominous whistling sound! A bomb!

"Take cover!"

"Hit the deck!"

Multiple shouts rang out as everyone ran for cover.

Boom! An ear-deafening blast struck their encampment.

After a few moments, Bill slowly picked himself up from the ground where he'd been flung by the concussion of the blast. He shook his head to stop the ringing in his ears and quickly looked around to assess casualties. He was relieved. The guys all signaled they were fine.

Then he heard a sound that pierced his heart like a knife. A dog whimpering.

> Trixie is writhing in pain. Something is burning hot!
>
> She can't move.
>
> *Help me, Bill, please help me. It hurts.*

"Trixie's been hit!" shouted Bill.

"Trixie's been hit!" was repeated from soldier to soldier, as others yelled, "Get the jeep!" "Get her to the medic!"

Bill cradled his furry best friend in his arms, blood running from Trixie's leg onto his uniform, as Corporal Johnson pulled up in a jeep. Bill jumped in and they set off immediately. Some soldiers ran alongside as far as they could. Others were praying. A few allowed tears to flow—saved up since D-Day—while the rest wore faces of shock.

"It's okay, girl. Hold on, Trixie. Just hold on," Bill whispered urgently.

> Trixie is in more pain than she can ever remember.
> Everything seems blurry . . . as if she is fading away.
> Bill's voice is comforting . . . but she seems to be
> floating away from him . . .

"Hold on, Trixie! We're here," he said as the jeep stopped. Bill ran into the tent as fast as he could. Thank goodness, there was the doctor. "Trixie's been hit!"

The doctor wrinkled his face. "That's a dog. I treat soldiers, not dogs."

"Trixie *is* a soldier," said Bill forcefully, pausing for a moment. The doctor was unmoved. Bill turned and ran back to the jeep. It was no use arguing with the doctor.

"Let's go to headquarters," he snapped to Corporal Johnson.

The corporal gave him a look.

"We don't have time for protocol. Trixie is dying. We have to save her!"

Everyone knew the chain of command. Army protocol called for Bill to go to the first sergeant, who would go to the second lieutenant, who'd take it to the major, who'd contact the colonel.

"We're going to the colonel!" said Bill flatly.

Leaving Trixie in the arms of Corporal Johnson, Bill tore into headquarters, right up to the colonel. He was breathless. "Sir, sorry, sir, but Trixie's been hit in the bomb attack. She has heavy blood loss. She's dying. And the doc refuses to treat her."

The colonel's facial demeanor changed instantly.

"Sergeant. Go straight back to the medic. Trust me. When you get there, that doctor will take care of our Trixie!"

"Yes, sir," said Bill, rushing back to the jeep.

When Corporal Johnson braked the jeep at the medic's tent, the doctor was waiting outside. He said nothing, but gently took Trixie from Bill's arms, covered in blood, and ordered his team to get busy. "We've got to save this dog!" he commanded.

Trixie is fading in and out. People are lifting her.
Wiping her leg.

The pain becomes less as the medicine goes to
work. She closes her eyes.

Finally, the doctor called Bill to come in. Corporal
Johnson and others waiting anxiously came along too.

Bill's heart was in his throat. Questions raced through
his mind: *Is she all right? Will she survive?* He had said more
prayers in the last hour than any other time in his life.

Trixie smells him. Bill is coming! She manages a
whimper, just to let him know she made it.

Bill heard the sound. Instantly his eyes filled with tears
that ran down his cheeks in little rivulets. He had to blink
to see.

"She's going to be fine," said the doctor.

"Thank you, Doc," said Bill, bending down to kiss the
little terrier on the head, noting her bandaged leg.

"You're going to be fine, Trixie. Did you hear the doctor? You'll be back on duty in no time." He ran his fingers
through the fur on her forehead.

When Bill picks Trixie up, she gets that warm feeling.
Knowing she is loved.

As Bill raised her in his arms, he could see the bloody shrapnel in a bowl. *Thank you, God,* he thought.

The doctor instructed Bill to change the bandage daily. And to stay in touch with him.

Bill looked at the doctor and repeated, "Thank you. Thank you very much."

The doctor glanced downward, then back to meet Bill's eyes. "I'm sorry. When you first came in . . . I didn't understand."

Bill nodded. "Thank you, Doctor."

Looking to Trixie, Bill said, "You're going to be okay, girl." Then, glancing at Corporal Johnson, "We're going to take you on a very slow, non-bumpy ride back to your bed, right, Corporal?"

Everyone laughed.

🐾 🐾 🐾

The upcoming winter was particularly brutal in Europe. Bill's unit was to continue to provide a supply line to Patton's tanks, sometimes finding themselves having to dig their trucks out of the snow to keep going.

It was bitterly cold. Bill bundled up Trixie as best he could in the trucks that, by and large, were open on both sides, with no heat in the cab. Bill and his men wore every piece of clothing they had in order to stay as warm as possible.

That was when the Battle of the Bulge played out, the last major engagement of World War II. The Germans were trying to stop the Allied advance to Germany by dividing their forces in Belgium. General Patton's tanks led the fight against the Germans, which began ten days before Christmas and extended to the end of January.

More than one million Allied troops participated in the Battle of the Bulge—half were Americans—and some forty thousand soldiers were killed or reported missing in action.

Enemy losses were worse. At the end of January, the Allied forces broke through and occupied Berlin. The war ended eight months later.

🐾　🐾　🐾

Warm weather had finally arrived when the first sergeant asked Bill to gather his men together. "I've got good news for you," he said with a slight pause, looking at the expectant young faces. "You're going home." Every face burst into a grin, cheering.

Bill looked at Trixie. "We're going home, girl! We're going home!"

Trixie looks at Bill's happy face. That is enough for her to start her tail wagging! But, this time, there is

something more. Bill—and all the men—are giving
off vibrations of unusual happiness! She decides to
show her happiness too . . . by dancing around in a
circle. They all laugh.

Days later Bill and his group were once again on the docks of Southampton, England. Right where the little pup named Trixie had dropped a stone on Bill's boot to get his attention.

Bill looked down at Trixie as he thought about that moment that seemed so long ago. He smiled at her and said, "We've been through a lot together, girl, haven't we?"

One of his men, looking on, made an innocent statement that crushed Bill to the quick.

"Too bad you can't take her home."

"What? What do you mean?" snapped Bill.

The man backed off a bit. "Sorry. I'm just saying . . . they're not going to let you take a dog on a ship."

Other guys started saying the same thing.

Bill felt panic. His body went numb. He had never considered this possibility. He couldn't just leave Trixie here! That would be like leaving your best friend behind.

His mind began racing, trying to figure out what to do. He said a silent prayer. *God, what do I do?* Then, just when they were told to move along and start boarding, he got a sudden idea! He began pulling clothes out of his duffel bag.

Other guys got the idea. They started stuffing Bill's things into their bags.

He leaned down, pointing to his bag. "Get in, girl, and stay very quiet. Don't make a sound."

> Trixie is confused. Why is Bill pointing to the bag?
>
> Then she gets the idea. Jump in and be quiet.
>
> *Zip!* She is in the dark. They are moving.

"Morris, William A. Jr., 20266."

Bill heard his name called and ran up the gangplank. Before long he had a room assignment with other guys and they all swore to keep their stowaway a secret.

Once the transport ship was out to sea, it was safe to let Trixie have the run of the ship. Which she did. And nobody questioned it.

> Trixie soon introduced herself to just about everyone on board the ship, always making it back to Bill in time to crawl into bed next to him.
>
> She enjoys the fresh sea air, loves the fond attention of all on board, and is particularly grateful

that this boat ride is so much more fun than the last
one she took . . . on D-Day.

Toward the end of the journey she can tell that Bill
is beginning to worry about something.

Bill confided to Corporal Johnson that he was worried
about their destination, Fort Dix, New Jersey. "It has a reputation for being one of the most prejudiced and abusive
bases to black soldiers in the country."

Corporal Johnson agreed.

"I'm not worried about me—it's Trixie I'm concerned
about. They'll kill her just because she belongs to me."

Corporal Johnson felt his pain, but he didn't know how
to comfort his friend. He didn't have a single idea how to
help.

As the outline of land began to form on the horizon,
Bill should have been excited about landing in America;
instead, his head was spinning, trying to figure out how he
could avoid taking Trixie to Fort Dix. He did the only thing
he knew how to do at times like these. He prayed.

Trixie doesn't like seeing Bill troubled. She can
always sense it.

She does the only thing she knows how to
do at times like these. She licks his hand. Letting

him know she loves him. Everything will be
all right.

As the ship began to pull up to the pier, the soldiers
stood at the railing, speculating where they were docking.

"Is this Fort Dix?"

"I don't know."

"Doesn't look like I thought New Jersey would look."

Bill's eyes widened. He read the sign. "Pouch Terminal."

"No way! This is not New Jersey. This is Staten Island,
New York. My folks live just a mile or so from here!" he
shouted.

He wondered if his prayer was being answered. If so,
how? His eyes scanned the dock, wondering if there was a
way to get Trixie off the ship and into the hands of someone who could take her home. But of course there wasn't.
Even though the gangplank was being lowered, any soldier
who left the ship without permission would be AWOL and
could be brought up on charges.

In the military, being absent without leave was severely
punishable. *What can I do? What can I do to save Trixie, God?*

Bill could see that most of the workers on the dock were
women, loading and unloading supplies on hand trucks.
During wartime, women took up the slack of men's jobs.

In that instant Bill saw her . . . Helen . . . a friend from high school, pushing a hand truck through the crowds on the dock. Bill shouted, "Helen! Helen!"

The others around him joined him—not knowing why—in a virtual chorus of cries to Helen. But she never responded.

On impulse, Bill swept up Trixie and said to the guys, "Keep yelling to Helen. This is my only chance."

He ran down to the lower level. Workers were now coming and going on the gangplank. Bill ran among them. The moment his feet touched the dock he knew he was AWOL.

His eyes scanned the crowd. *Where did she go? Help me find her, God!* Then he spotted her about to disappear into a warehouse. "Helen!"

Bill's loud yell blended perfectly with the shouts from the boat: "Helen!"

She quickly turned around, wearing a confused look on her face, just as Bill ran up to her.

"Helen!" said Bill breathlessly.

"Bill? Is that you?"

"Yes, it's me."

Her countenance broke into a wide smile of surprise.

"And who is this . . . the famous Trixie?"

Bill was momentarily stunned. "You know Trixie?"

"Ha! All of Staten Island has probably heard about your soldier dog from Norcie!"

Bill was overwhelmed. Then he remembered . . . he was AWOL!

"Helen. I'm not supposed to be off the ship. I'm trying to save Trixie's life. Can you take her to Norcie? Or my mom?" Without waiting for an answer, he kissed Trixie on the head, fought off tears, and handed her to Helen. And, without missing a beat, he turned and ran back toward the ship.

"Yes, I will!" she shouted . . . to his back. Laughing.

He turned his head slightly and yelled over his shoulder: "And tell 'em I love 'em. Will call as soon as I can!"

Bill was almost to the gangplank.

He soon was able to blend in, helping a worker push a cart up the ramp, trying to look like he was supposed to be doing that. Once onto the ship, he strolled along the deck, whistling, as if everything was fine and dandy. Actually, it was! Trixie was safe and she'd get to see his family before he did. Once again, he whispered a *Thank you* to God.

He ventured a glance to the dock. He saw Helen, cradling Trixie. The pup was looking over her shoulder as she was swallowed by the crowd.

> Trixie is looking and looking for Bill.
>
> *Why did he run away like that? Why did he leave me with this lady?*

Several hours later the bus carrying Bill and the other soldiers pulled up to the guard house at Fort Dix. They were directed to their barracks.

Unfortunately, the base's widely held reputation for prejudice was soon evident. White soldiers, just back from the war, got to relax, play Ping-Pong, and await their official discharge. However, Bill and his men were ordered to carry out menial tasks like taking out the trash and picking up litter.

Bill said to his guys, "Just keep telling yourself . . . we're home. We won't be here very long."

It was a week before he could get to a phone. He knew Norcie would be at work, so he called his mother, Susie Morris. He was thrilled to hear her voice.

"Mom, it's me, Junior! I'm in Fort Dix. Coming home soon. How's Trixie?"

It immediately occurred to him that he may have sounded insensitive . . . instead of asking how *she* was, he asked about his dog. Then he remembered something else. "Mom, don't let Trixie around any kids. In the war we trained her not to trust kids . . . agents of the enemy."

His mom let out a loud, loving laugh. Oh, what a wonderful sound. He always looked forward to her laugh, especially at the Sunday dinner table.

"Junior, your little dog started playing with kids in the

neighborhood the moment she arrived! They love her, and she loves them. That's some doggie you have. But Trixie is with Norcie, and Norcie tells everyone that if she can't have her husband yet, Trixie's the next best thing!" She laughed loudly again.

Bill asked how his dad, brothers, and sisters were doing; told his mom that he really missed her; and confessed that his stomach had been saving a place for her cooking for more than a year!

He said, "I better go, Mom. Tell Norcie I love her and miss her. I hope to get my discharge soon."

🐾 🐾 🐾

One week later Trixie is snoozing in the apartment that Norcie shares with her sisters.

Suddenly she jumps up. It is as if every nerve in her body sent her a message at the same moment. She can feel him! She can smell him! And . . . she can hear him!

Footsteps on the porch . . . those are Bill's!

Bill was pleased. Norcie still hid the key in the same place. Before he could even slip it into the lock, he heard whimpering and scratching from the other side.

He walked in to see Trixie barking and dancing in circles, her tail wagging like crazy.

"Trixie, I'm home." She leaped about three feet right into his arms, licking his face and ears. Bill hugged his best friend and they rolled around on the floor, a pandemonium of laughing and barking.

They didn't even realize they had an audience. Norcie and her sisters came home right after Bill and were just standing there taking it all in. They were laughing too.

Norcie was next to jump into Bill's outstretched arms. Bill twirled her around, lifting her feet off the floor, as he planted that kiss he'd been saving up through D-Day, the Battle of the Bulge, and many other adventures. The sisters would never forget the joy they witnessed that day on Staten Island . . . the reunion of a man and his wife, and a man and his dog.

🐾 🐾 🐾

Bill, Norcie, and Trixie moved into a large apartment above the Morris Moving Company office, and soon they were back into the swing of life at home, working hard all week at their jobs, Norcie in nursing and Bill back behind the wheel of Morris Moving trucks. And then, the highlight of the week, Sunday dinner at his parents' house.

Trixie has a new job too. She goes to work with Bill
every day. If she isn't in the front seat of the truck
next to him, she is stationed at her favorite place in
the office, a little rug near the desk belonging to Bill's
dad, William.

Phones are always ringing, people coming and
going, and they need to be greeted in a friendly
manner. It all keeps Trixie very busy.

One day Bill lifted Trixie up and sat her in his lap as he
and Norcie were about to make an announcement.

"Up till now, Trixie, you've been our special member
of the family. After what we went through on the battle-
fields of Europe and somehow survived, then we came back
home and became a family . . . you, me, and Norcie." Bill
ran his hand through Trixie's fur and looked her right in the
eyes to see that she was listening.

"But . . ." He paused. "Now our family is growing! Right
this minute . . . inside Norcie."

Norcie flashed her million-dollar smile, watching her
husband go through this ritual. "Norcie's having a baby!"

Trixie takes her cue. She leaps from Bill's lap
and dances around the floor, barking and
wagging her tail.

It is wonderful news! She isn't sure what it

means . . . but she always knows when it is
wonderful news!

When baby Dolores was born a few months later, Trixie
had a new station: right under the crib.

> Babies fill the house with new smells. Some are a
> little pungent, but most are pleasant. Trixie loves the
> smell of baby powder on little Dolores.
>
> And she loves the evolution of the sounds . . .
> first, from the gurgling of a baby, to the cooing
> and imitative expressions of an infant, to a toddler
> speaking words, laughing, and—the most fun—being
> a playmate.
>
> Still, Trixie doesn't let her guard down. There
> are huge moving vans traveling on the road that
> runs in front of the Morris Moving Company
> office and Bill and Norcie's apartment. That spells
> danger.

Dolores and Trixie were buddies through her "terrible
twos." But, in the same way that Trixie had once listened
for enemy soldiers to keep Bill safe during the war, the pup
was always on high alert around Dolores.

Bill and Norcie got a kick out of Trixie's watchfulness. It
also gave them—particularly Norcie—assurance that Do-

lores had a furry guardian angel. For example, Norcie was comfortable putting baby Dolores into her playpen, in the sunshine, in the fenced-in side yard—she knew that Trixie was always on duty.

However, neither Norcie nor Bill had realized that toddler Dolores had secretly developed an advanced talent in escape artistry. No one could say how long she'd been plotting to scale the playpen and escape.

>Trixie has been napping next to the playpen.
>
>*What? Where did the baby go?!*
>
>Trixie leaps to all fours, sniffing the ground, following the scent to the backyard gate—which Dolores had somehow opened! *Oh no!* Following her nose, Trixie races around to the front of the house.
>
>Toddler Dolores is marching rapidly to the end of the driveway. Alarm bells sound inside Trixie! They are saying, *Big trucks . . . watch out!*

Just as the child was about to step onto the road, into the path of an oncoming truck, something grabbed her pants and pulled her back! Now she was being dragged up the driveway! Dolores shouted at Trixie: "Stop, Trixie, stop!"

Trixie isn't going to listen to toddler Dolores
until she is safe. She refuses to let go of the child's
pant leg, thereby preventing her from getting up.

Norcie had the window open and suddenly heard her
child screaming, "Stop, Trixie, stop!"

She bolted out the door, and saw the playpen empty
and the gate open. Her heart pounded as she rounded the
corner to find her little girl shouting for Trixie to let go.

The moment Norcie arrives, Trixie does let go,
allowing Mom to take over. Whew!

Norcie cuddled Dolores in her arms and walked back
into the house, saying, "Don't cry, Trixie was just keeping
you safe. You're not hurt. Just your feelings."

Trixie decides it is time for a rest. This secret
service work with a precocious toddler is almost
as harrowing as crossing the English Channel in the
front seat of a truck, next to Bill, being shot at by
machine guns!

Two days later at Sunday dinner, Bill's dad, William, made
certain that everyone heard the story of Trixie's heroism.

William sat at the head of the table and surveyed the brothers, sisters, spouses, and children around him. Bill's mom, Susie, aided by a couple of daughters, placed heaping platters of turkey, mashed potatoes, gravy, and greens on the table.

When everyone was seated, and grace had been said, William pointed to the "Hero of the Day," Trixie—who was sitting on a chair right between Bill and himself—and asked Norcie to tell everyone about the biggest event of the week.

Norcie flashed her wonderful smile and began telling the hair-raising story of Trixie saving Dolores from stepping into traffic on their busy street.

After that, William asked Bill to once again tell the family a story of heroism from his and Trixie's time at war.

No one ever tired of hearing the story of a pup who picked out a single soldier from among ten thousand and remained at his side from D-Day to the Battle of the Bulge.

And, yes, now that they were safely at home, Bill loved to share the heroic story of Trixie the soldier dog who alerted Bill about advancing enemy soldiers before taking down the enemy soldier who would have otherwise shot Bill or Corporal Johnson.

Trixie never understands all the words, but she can tell when they are talking about her. It makes her feel closer to her number one . . . Bill.

She loves him . . . most of all.

And Bill loves her.

Reflections

The Godwinks and dogwinks of the Trixie story are never-ending. Without the divine alignment of Bill and Trixie—being at the right place at exactly the right time as protectors of each other—it's hard to imagine them surviving the horrific experience of war.

The continuing dogwinks, once they returned home to America, seemed to confirm that dogs are angelic agents of God Himself.

> *Who gives us more understanding*
> *than the animals of the earth.*
> —JOB 35:11*

---

* New American Standard Bible.

🐾   🐾   🐾

Trixie lived to be sixteen years old. She was laid to rest behind the Morris Moving Company offices.

This condensed story was adapted from the book by Dolores Morris, *The Soldier That Wagged Her Tail*, the true story of her dad, Bill Morris, and Trixie.

12

HUNTER

HMMM . . . that smells good, thinks the pup. He is still getting used to his new home, and a brand-new name.

"Hunter, do you like spaghetti sauce?" asked Tim.

The husky pup looks up at Tim from his spot, under the kitchen table. *What's spaaa-get-tea?* he wonders.

"With our head colds, he's probably the only one who can smell it," said Jill, Tim's wife, stirring the pot and turning the gas down to simmer.

Tim, also congested, sniffed the air; he couldn't smell a

thing. "True enough," he said, and shrugged, reaching to rub Hunter's head.

Hunter looks up at Tim: I like that.

"Girls, time to eat!" shouted Jill, and then the family's two younger daughters swirled to the dining room table, just off the kitchen. Thirteen-year-old Alyssa and her eight-year-old sister, Sarah, took their seats. Ashley, sixteen, came into the kitchen, getting drinks for herself and her sisters.

"Hi, Hunter," she said, passing the pup on the floor.

Hunter looks up. It's been two weeks to the day since he was in that cage at the shelter and that very girl had said, "How about this one?"

Hunter had no way of knowing that the family, at the time, was still recovering from the loss of another dog. Jill had taken it the hardest; that dog was "her baby."

Two Weeks Earlier

Tim McLarty knew his dear wife was still hurting. He thought if they got another dog, it would help her through the grieving process.

"I don't think I can do that right now," she had told him, saying that she'd considered—and dismissed—that possibility.

But when the photo of a cute-as-can-be husky named Charles popped up on the Pet Store website, Tim tried again.

"Just look at this face," he coaxed his wife, pointing to the picture on the screen.

She gave him a long stare, as if to say, *Are you still at it?* But . . . thinking about the rest of the family . . . she reconsidered and caved. "Oh, okay."

The Pet Store was arranged with multiple cages along the walls, each with a hand-printed card naming the occupant.

"There's Charles!" shouted Alyssa excitedly. And there he was, a husky puppy causing all five of the McLartys to simultaneously move toward the cage, expressing their uniform feelings: "Awwww."

"Can we get him, Mommy?" Sarah jumped, gleefully.

"Wellll . . ." Jill began, secretly thinking that this little dog was already stealing her heart.

"Oh, I'm sorry, that puppy has already been taken," said an apologetic voice from behind, a saleslady whose mission was to attach a new sign—"I've Been Adopted!"—to Charles's cage.

The McLartys uniformly slumped.

Hey, what about me? That's the attitude of the puppy
one cage to the left of Charles, another husky, black
with a white chest and forepaws. He jumps up and
down to get someone's attention.

"How about this one?" said Ashley, waving everyone
over. "His name is Ray."

"That's the brother," offered the saleslady. "Two little
brothers, Ray and Charles."

The cleverness that someone had named the sibling puppies after famous soul singer Ray Charles went right over
the heads of the kids. But Tim and Jill got it. They smiled.

"These two little guys are huskies," continued the
saleslady.

"How big will he get?" asked Tim cautiously.

"Probably thirty to fifty pounds," she replied.

🐾　🐾　🐾

An hour later the McLartys were back home, enthusiasti-
cally gabbing about their newest family member. "What
should we call him?" asked Tim. They all started throwing
out names—presumably something more suitable for a dog
than "Ray."

Ashley was quiet. She was pondering, trying to identify

someone she liked who had a really unique name. Not just a name, but a name that *said* something and fit this dog. A thought suddenly zipped into her mind . . . a singer she'd recently been listening to, Hunter Hayes.

"Hey, I got it!" All conversations stopped. "Hunter."

They thought about it and everyone agreed. Hunter was a great name for a great husky dog.

> *What in the dickens are they talking about?* wonders
> the pup on the floor, who for the last few moments
> had watched a ping-pong game of people shouting
> out names. Now they are all staring at him.

"Hi, Hunter," they said, with various inflections. "Do you like that name?"

> He doesn't really know how to answer. But he's
> learned, when in doubt, to stand up and wag
> your tail. So, that's what he does.

When it was time to go to bed, Jill put Hunter into his cage off the kitchen and turned down the lights.

> Hunter doesn't like being alone in the dark.
> He begins to whine. As loudly as he can.

Nothing happens. So, he keeps on whining. And
whining.

Snap. Hunter hears the kitchen light flick on. There
is Jill in her jammies. *Uh-oh,* he thinks, freezing his
position. *Am I in trouble?*

"Oh, okay . . . you can come with us," said Jill, opening
the cage door.

Hunter's response is instant. Stand up and wag!
Then, *Wow, she's cuddling me!*

Moments later he was in a nice spot at the bottom of a
big bed in which Jill and Tim were sound asleep.

Two Weeks Later

By now the husky pup had had fourteen days to get to
know his new family. And boy, did he love them.

Hunter lies at the end of the bed, listening to the
breathing of his two owners in a deep sleep—
slightly more raspy because of their head colds.

He realizes that he has it pretty doggone good. Since that first night, he's never again had to go into that cage. He even noticed that Tim had stuck it in the garage, out of the way.

Yep, this is a loving home. I get to sleep here, they treat me nice, and feed me well.

He thinks about that delicious cooking smell earlier, whatever Jill had been making for dinner. *What did Tim call it? Oh yeah, spaaa-get-tea.*

Hunter sniffs. *Wait. That's not spaaa-get-tea.* There is another odor. Something pungent. He cocks his head.

The clock on the nightstand said 12:00 a.m. The house was quiet: Jill and Tim asleep in the master bedroom upstairs; the two youngest girls in another bedroom upstairs; and Ashley downstairs in the first-floor bedroom.

Hunter springs up. *Something's wrong!* He begins to run back and forth on the bed, trying to get Jill's or Tim's attention. He jumps up and down.

"Hunter, what's going on?" said Jill, slightly dazed. Hunter stopped, looked at her, and whined.

"Shhh . . . you'll wake everybody up," said Jill in a loud whisper. "Lie down. Go back to sleep."

Jill laid her head back on the pillow.

> Hunter realizes he isn't getting through to her! Isn't Jill smelling what he is?
>
> He leaps to the floor and begins running back and forth, making enough commotion to again get Jill's attention.

"Hunter!" she said, sitting up, realizing this was very unusual. Lifting her legs out of bed, she asked in a concerned voice, "What's the matter, boy?"

At that, Hunter bolted to the top of the stairs. Stopped, looked back, then headed downstairs.

She jumped from the bed to follow him, down the stairs and into the kitchen.

As Jill came into the kitchen, she flipped the switch to the lights, seeing Hunter standing at the stove.

She finally smelled it! Through her stuffy nose, she could now clearly smell the distasteful odor of gas! She noticed the burner. It was still on "simmer," but the flame had gone out!

"Tim!" she yelled as she quickly grasped the knob and turned off the burner.

In moments Tim was bouncing down the stairs, also smelling the deadly gas.

"Open the doors and windows!" he shouted. Jill was already ahead of him, flinging open the back door. They grabbed towels, whipping them in the air to dissipate the dangerous fumes.

A few minutes later, crisis averted, they plopped down at the kitchen table and just looked at each other. Everything was now quiet. Everything in order. No one else there. The girls apparently had slept right through the emergency.

They began to assess what had occurred.

"What if there had been a spark when I flipped the lights on?" asked Jill incredulously, looking at her husband wide-eyed. He, equally astonished, slowly shook his head, as if to say, *I don't even want to think about it!*

He turned back to her. "Think about this. What if Hunter hadn't been insistent about getting you up?"

"What if, two weeks ago, we'd brought home a different dog . . . not Hunter?"

"He's our hero!" they said in unison.

They both looked around the kitchen.

"Where's Hunter?" they said simultaneously, jumping up, looking around downstairs, then going upstairs.

There he was. At the foot of the bed. Job done. Sound asleep. No doubt dreaming about spaaa-get-tea!

Reflections

Consider the Godwink/dogwink: it was two weeks to the day that the McLartys brought home a new member of the family, Hunter, a pup they'd chosen because the dog they wanted was already adopted. And this night, he had quite possibly saved their home and their lives.

They were divinely protected by a gift from God in the form of a dog named Hunter—the pup they rescued, who rescued them.

13

BELLA

The blond-haired toddler was bewildered. Her mother's eyes were watery and her voice cracked as she repeated, in German: "You know I love you. I will always love you."

Looking at her longingly, the mother handed the child a stuffed animal. "Whenever you hug this little doggie," she whispered, attempting to keep her composure, "think of me. Please?"

The mother turned her head to hide the tears that poured from her eyes. Then she was gone.

Sonja soon had new parents. They were nice to her. And she grew to love them. But, like wisps of vapor, those final moments with her birth mother were always there, floating in the back of her mind.

Years passed.

Sonja Harper, now forty-eight years old, looked around the Texas backyard barbecue to see if she knew anyone, other than the friend who'd invited her, who was busily chatting with other friends.

Not a soul, she thought.

Something nudged her ankle. She looked down.

The face of the cutest black poodle was looking back at her, its tail wagging.

Hello, would you like a friend? I need one too.

Sonja kneeled down to pet the friendly pup. "Hello there. Are you having a good time at the party? Do you like having all these visitors at your home?"

"That's my daughter's dog."

Sonja turned toward the friendly woman's voice; she spoke with a charming southern accent.

She stood up, smiling. "What a cutie-pie. Male or female?"

"Her name is Skella," said the woman, her voice turning sad. "But we're going to miss her. My daughter is off to college and we need to find this sweet pup a new home." Then, looking directly at Sonja, she asked, "Would you like to take her home with you?"

"Ahhhh . . ." Sonja was caught off guard. "Well . . . you

know . . . a friend recently suggested I get a dog, but I work . . . and I couldn't bear the thought of going to a shelter and having to pick out just one." She laughed nervously.

"Skella's such a dear . . . She's had all her shots . . . and we have a cage we can give you."

Sonja was feeling waves of indecision. She was also feeling a nudging at her ankles again. Apparently, somebody else was trying to convince her . . . the little black poodle herself!

She'd just moved into a new apartment . . . she was a single working mother . . . her kids were all out on their own . . . *Do I want the responsibility?*

> The little pup chimes in, jumps up and down, and
> wags her tail.

"Well, it looks like Skella likes the idea," said the lady.

A short while later Skella rested her head on Sonja's lap as they drove home, the cage and other paraphernalia taking up most of the back seat.

As she drove, something was on her mind; was it indecision? *Am I making a mistake, bringing a pet into my life at this point?* She couldn't put a finger on what was haunting her.

Forcing herself to change thoughts, Sonja glanced down

and began talking with the pup. "I think we have to get you a new name," she said, wrinkling her forehead in thought. She was quiet for a minute or two, mulling over choices.

Skella just looked at Sonja, listening, as if she understood every word.

"I got it!" Sonja said excitedly. "Bella rhymes with Skella . . . but Bella means beautiful. And you are a beautiful girl!" Sonja tousled Skella's head. "How do you like that name, Bella? You like Bella?"

Bella wags her tail, happy to agree with whatever Sonja is saying.

Still . . . something continued to nag at Sonja . . . what was it?

Arriving at her new apartment, Sonja held Bella's leash with one hand while lugging the cage from the car. Inside, she filled a bowl with water, placed it on the kitchen floor, and gave Bella a tour of her new home: the living room, the bathroom, and the two bedrooms.

In the second bedroom, which also served as Sonja's workroom, there were shelves filled with books and memorabilia.

"Oh, look what's here, Bella!" Sonja said brightly. "This is the toy that my mommy gave me . . . the last time I saw her."

Instantly her eyes filled with tears as she held the stuffed animal, the last physical connection to her birth mother before being placed into adoption. She could now remember additional words her mother tearfully spoke so long ago: "I can no longer take care of you . . . your new parents will give you a safe and loving home . . ."

> Bella looks up at Sonja, sensing that something very sad is going on.

Sonja now grasped the toy animal, holding it tightly to her chest, her tears spilling down upon it, as they had so many times before.

The moving images in her mind became clearer. In all earlier times she was unable to make out her mother's face . . . but now, for an instant, she did. She saw her mother hand her the toy and heard, "I will always love you."

In that moment, God gave her eyes to see an endearing Godwink . . . putting it all together! The tattered and worn toy given to her by her mother nearly fifty years before was a poodle . . . a little black poodle. Just like Bella!

A feeling of unexpected joy washed over Sonja. It was a Godwink confirmation.

> Bella senses something has changed for the better.
> She stands tall, wagging her tail in full agreement!

Reflections

For the first time Sonja was able to tap deeply into her childhood memory to recall the voice and the face of her mother.

Godwinks can do that: allow you to see things previously unseen; hear things previously unheard.

When it happens, you know that God has been with you all along—yesterday, today, and He will be with you tomorrow.

14

MOE I

"You can never give back as much love as a dog gives you," said Chuck McCann, a comedic film and TV actor with a friendly, boyish face. He was reminiscing about the mongrel black Labrador retriever and beagle that once rode next to him in his truck.

"The first time I saw him, there was almost a pileup on Ventura Boulevard," recalled Chuck, describing the morning he left a breakfast meeting in Studio City, California, just as a spry, undersized black Lab bounced into traffic.

"I pulled my truck diagonally across the street, blocking traffic, making sure he wasn't hit, and watched him dart down an alley."

Then, leaving a cacophony of beeping horns behind, he drove down the one-lane street looking for the little dog.

The pup, frightened by the near miss with a car and all the beeping horns, ran as fast as he could, past trash cans and parked cars that lined the alley adjacent to the backs of buildings.

> The dog is so rattled he darts right past the
> alluring, mouth-watering odors behind a Chinese
> restaurant. Through an intersection, up a side
> street, and down some steps, into a park. Finally,
> panting, he halts. Looks around. Has no idea
> where he is.

Chuck pulled his truck to the curb, hopped out, and rapidly descended some steps into a park. He slipped and fell.

"Ow."

Sprawled on the steps, he pulled up a pant leg to assess the injury—a skinned knee. He dabbed it with a handkerchief. And he felt a wet, cold tongue run across his cheek.

"Hey there, fella. I'm okay. Are you okay? C'mon with me . . . we'll see if we can get you back home."

> The little dog jumps into the truck right next to the
> man whose low, reassuring voice comforts him.

The man introduces himself as Chuck and talks to him all the way to his house.

Hey . . . this isn't bad! Chuck and his wife, Betty, fill up a big bowl with food, next to another one with cool water.

The pup looks up when Chuck says, "Smile!" He hears a click from the black thing that Chuck is pointing at him. Chuck then shows it to him. *That's me . . . inside that black thing!* He has no idea he's just had his picture taken.

A short while later Chuck said, "C'mon, pup, we're going to see if we can find your family." With a stack of papers under his arm, he opened the truck door and lifted the dog up.

Chuck and the pup traveled from neighborhood to neighborhood plastering posters on trees, light poles, and fences. "Found: Small Black Lab" was written under a picture of the dog, asking people to call if they had any information.

The next day Chuck received a phone call. A lady said the dog sounded like a mutt that she too had once found and returned to its owner. She had a number. Chuck called it, leaving a message on the answering machine saying that he may have found their dog.

Six days passed.

Finally, a woman telephoned. "Yeah, that sounds like our dog," she said in a monotone voice, devoid of emotion. "We were moving to a new house. He was playing in the yard. Guess he must've run off."

"What's his name?" asked Chuck, with a slight trace of annoyance at the woman's lack of concern.

"Moe."

Chuck turned from the phone and yelled, "Moe!"

At that instant, the black Lab lifted his head and dashed toward the sound of Chuck's voice.

> Moe looks up at Chuck as if to say, *Excuse me, sir, did you call me?*
>
> When Chuck calls his name a second time, Moe responds by dancing a jig, running in circles, and jumping up and down. His tail is wagging so fast it creates a breeze!

"Yep. This is your dog," said Chuck. "Didn't you get my message from last week?"

"Yesss . . ." said the woman with some hesitancy, "but we were moving, and I thought he'd be all right where he was."

Chuck stared at the phone.

"Ma'am, if you don't want the dog, I'll keep him."

"All right," she drawled.

That was how Moe came to be Chuck's permanent best friend. They were inseparable. Everywhere Chuck went, Moe went. And Moe always had his favorite spot in the truck—right next to Chuck.

Moe loves Chuck. He is so grateful for that time, long ago, when Chuck tracked him down . . . hurting his knee, after he'd blocked the traffic to let him safely cross the busy road.

A dog has many ways to show appreciation. Licking Chuck's face is the most obvious. But coming to him, whenever he calls, and snuggling up to him whenever he can, are two more.

He likes it when Chuck tells other people, "This is Moe. My best pal."

They were best pals for ten years.

Then one day Moe seemed to be out of sorts. He wasn't his normal, friendly, frisky self. Instead of jumping up when Chuck came into the room, he stayed where he was. Looking sad.

"What's the matter, Moe boy? We've got to get you to the doctor."

Moe doesn't know why, but he just doesn't have the energy to do things he likes to do.

It is now too hard for him to jump up on the bed,
to lie down next to Chuck and Betty. He wishes he
didn't have to, but . . . he has to wait for Chuck to
help him up.

"It's a stomach disorder," explained the vet. "All we can do is prescribe medication to try to prevent the disease from spreading."

Chuck was worried. And he knew he was only buying time. During the following year, Chuck sadly watched the slow deterioration of his beloved dog.

"I'm sorry," said the vet. "We've done all we can."

A constriction swelled in Chuck's throat as tears filled his eyes. Hearing the inevitable news struck him like a ton of bricks.

Moe seems to sleep most of the time. He wants
to jump up, like he used to, every time Chuck says,
"Let's go for a ride, pal." But he just doesn't have the
energy.

He wishes he could still run and jump like the
good old days.

But, meanwhile, sleeping here in Chuck's arms . . .
that's pretty comforting.

It was the saddest time Chuck could ever remember—with Moe cradled in his arms, tears streaming down his cheeks.

This time Moe went to sleep. And never woke up.

🐾   🐾   🐾

The next ten months of mourning were unbearable. Every time Chuck climbed into his truck, he missed Moe scrambling to be at his side. Every time he walked to the door, he missed Moe jumping up to accompany him. Every time he climbed into bed, he missed the weight of Moe leaping in behind him.

Chuck and Betty now had other dogs. Four of them—all rescued, one way or another. They were all nice dogs. But . . . he really missed Moe.

One Saturday afternoon, Chuck and Betty were driving with a friend who asked if they could stop by Johnny Carson Park. He wanted to see someone.

As they walked into the park, a dog adoption event was going on. Various rescue groups had set up tables and little tents and were looking for new homes for animals. As Chuck, Betty, and their friend passed a booth featuring Lhasa apsos, Chuck paused for a moment. One particular dog came right up to him.

"He's like a small bag of feathers," said Chuck with surprise, lifting the tiny dog with soft fur and a cute face that belonged on a stuffed toy.

He felt a warm, indescribable connection with the dog. He brought him up close and spotted something unusual: the dog had one blue eye and one brown.

"This is the cutest dog I've ever seen," said Chuck to a lady with the rescue group. "What's his name?"

"Moe."

The world stopped! Or so it seemed. Chuck was astonished. He momentarily stared at the woman.

"What did you say?"

"His name is Moe," she repeated.

Chuck and Betty couldn't believe their ears.

"I . . . I've got to have this dog," he said.

The lady smiled, shrugging slightly. "Put your name on the list," she said perfunctorily. "About a hundred others also want him."

"But, I've got to have this dog," Chuck insisted. "Honest . . . we'd provide a wonderful home for him. Look! Look how we've bonded," he said, stroking the dog's soft little head.

Unaccustomed to such persistence, the woman began asking questions.

"Well . . . where would he sleep?" she asked doubtfully.

"On my bed, of course," replied Chuck, with an air of wouldn't-everybody-know-that. "We have a house built for dogs. They just let us stay there," continued Chuck, trying to score some points with humor. "They have their own door. They come and go as they please into a dog run. Please . . . come visit our home . . . see for yourself."

Later that day, that's just what the lady did.

Satisfied that Chuck and Betty could indeed provide a wonderful home, the woman placed the little Lhasa apso with one blue eye and one brown into Chuck's arms—a little six-month-old "bag of feathers" with the unbelievable name of Moe.

"I'll always miss my first Moe," said Chuck, "but this little Moe is filling a big hole in my heart."

Reflections

Grief is one of the most difficult paths to navigate in life. We may think we are ready. In fact, intellectually, we may *be* ready. But rarely are we prepared for the emotional burden that seems to be thrust upon us, to be carried all of a sudden, all by ourselves.

The loss of a pet is a weight upon our hearts that can feel just as heavy as the loss of another member of the family.

Just as Chuck grieved the loss of his pal Moe, your dog may have had extraordinary attributes that were missed even more than those from humans.

The unconditional love your dog demonstrated, over and over, meant that there was never a list of grievances kept against you. Maybe you didn't always come home when you said you would, or you sometimes lost your temper. Your pet still loved you . . . without conditions.

The special connection the two of you developed over the years will never be broken. But your memories of the love and loyalty they showed you can be relived by recalling the many Godwinks and dogwinks you shared together.

15

MOE II

Krista Clark was in one of the worst states of her life. She was recently divorced, had a horrible boss, and hadn't been speaking to her parents for months.

Worse, she was approaching the first anniversary of the loss of Jaeger, her 105-pound yellow Labrador. Her relationship with that dear dog had been very special. He was the sweetest, most lovable dog on earth. He had brought her and her family so much joy.

The first anniversary of losing a loved one is always dreaded. Like watching an approaching storm cloud, hoping it will pass uneventfully, but fearing it will erupt, leaving us drenched in uncontrollable emotion.

Krista could never have imagined how long the mourning period would last.

"With everything piling up, I was becoming a hermit, miserable and sinking deeper every day," she recalls.

One day Krista was chatting with her friend and chiropractor J.P., talking about life, how hard it was, and how hopeless she was feeling.

At the end of her appointment, her chiropractor handed her a slip of paper. Krista looked at it. In neat handwriting were the titles of three books about Godwinks.

Krista looked at her questioningly.

"Whenever I'm feeling down, I read these books."

Krista thanked J.P. and stuffed the paper in her pocket.

Barnes & Noble was on her way home, so she pulled in, parked her car, and went to the customer service counter. A young man took her scrap of paper and soon returned with the three books.

For the next week, Krista read several stories each night before bed.

"I began to feel like a huge burden was being lifted. I felt better and was even able to smile!" she wrote to J.P., again thanking her. "I am seeing the light at the end of the tunnel and believe I really am going to get through this . . . whatever 'this' is."

One evening she had a Godwink. The phone rang. It was her mother calling out of the blue, wanting to get together to talk and reconcile. Krista was cordial and told her mom that she'd think about it. And pray about it.

"If she'd called several days earlier, I would have refused," Krista later told J.P., "but after learning about the Godwinks in my life, I was beginning to face the music, make amends, and have amends made to me. It was beautiful!"

That night, thanking God and smiling, Krista opened up the last volume. She got a third of the way into the book and began reading the story about Moe and Chuck.

Moments later tears were streaming down her face. She couldn't believe it. She was reading this story on the very anniversary of her dog Jaeger's passing. She could totally identify with the feelings of loss by Chuck in the story about Moe.

The next day, Krista called her mother, asking if she could stop by after work.

She placed the Godwink books in a little gift bag and calculated her arrival at her parents' house for when she knew her dad would have gotten home.

Krista's parents were so pleased to see her. They held open their arms and hugged her. Tightly. For a long time.

After a little conversation, Krista said she had brought some books that she wanted to leave with them, suspecting they would enjoy them as much as she did.

She looked at them and said, "Is it okay if I read you one of my favorite stories?"

They both nodded agreeably.

She opened up to the story about Moe and read it aloud. It was a struggle for Krista to get through it.

In her entire life, she had had only a few glimpses of her father crying. This time she got more than a glimpse—he wept.

Her mother was sobbing, and by the end, there was a sort of *Wow* feeling at how God lets us know He is right there with us, guiding us and taking care of us. We just have to be ready to listen.

Krista realized that as much as the Moe and Chuck story had touched her heart, lifting much of the dread of facing the anniversary of the death of their yellow Lab, her parents also needed help with grief. In a way, they were still mourning not only Jaeger, but also the estrangement of their daughter.

"That day was a turning point," Krista told J.P. during a subsequent chiropractic appointment. "My parents wake up every morning, have their devotions, and read a Godwink story. We get on the phone and talk about the stories. And it tickles me to hear my dad asking people, 'What was your Godwink today?'"

It just goes to show the rippling effect of Godwinks in each of our lives. From Moe and Chuck's Godwink dogwinks—stretching across the miles, lifting the hopes of Krista at a difficult time in her life—to helping to repair a broken family.

Reflections

When we talk about Godwinks, we often ask, "What are the odds?"

Think about the odds Krista experienced. When she reached her low point, she was divinely aligned with the phenomenon of Godwinks through her chiropractor friend J.P.

What are the odds that just as Godwinks were opening Krista's heart to "receive amends," she gets a call from her mother asking for reconciliation?

Then, what are the odds that on the very anniversary of the passing of her sweet dog Jaeger, Krista would read the story about Moe and Chuck? The hope from that story helped lift her from her grief.

Finally, consider the odds: Godwinks became the thread of unity that helped knit her family relationships back together.

16

FAITH

It was a cold January afternoon in Oklahoma City as Jude looked out the front window to see her son, Reuben, and his friend Jon tossing a football. A moment later Reuben was heading into the house.

"Hey, Mom, can I borrow the car? I'm going to give Jon a ride home. And his dog had puppies in a field over near the flea market. We're going to check 'em out."

That was just like Reuben. The sweetest seventeen-year-old on earth; helping out a buddy, but even more, ready to help a dog in need.

Jude Stringfellow was a single mom who had taught her three teenagers, Reuben, Laura, and Caitlyn, to respect animals, especially dogs. They had two dogs of their own and occasionally took in others, as a foster home, all the

while keeping them secret from a landlord who forbade
pets.

Knowing her son's weakness, Jude flatly stated, "Don't
bring any puppies home. We have enough."

A short while later, the boys approached the split-rail
fence running behind the flea market.

"Princess!" called Jon, looking for his dog.

Reuben and Jon continued calling out her name, then
spotted the black Chow.

"There she is. I'll take a look," said Reuben, climbing
through the fence.

"Careful, she gets mean when she's birthing," observed
Jon.

"Hey, Princess," said Reuben gently as he approached
the mother dog lying in a corner, among the weeds.

Princess emitted a low *stay-away-from-here* growl.

"How many in the litter?" shouted Jon.

"About five or six nursing," said Reuben, trying not to
talk loudly. "Wait, there's another one in trouble!"

A small clump of fur, with just its back legs sticking out
from underneath the full weight of the mother dog, was
kicking, desperately trying to survive. The little pup's head
and forefront were being squished!

Ignoring the snarling sounds of Princess, Reuben grasped
the pup . . . a female . . . and pulled her out from under-

neath the mother dog, quickly tucking her under his foot-ball jersey.

Princess angrily showed her teeth.

He jumped back, now seeing that Princess was rising to attack him, and ran. He scrambled through the fence, leaving the mother dog barking and snarling on the other side as he and Jon ran away.

"Told ya she gets mean," said Jon when they stopped a safe distance away.

Reuben lifted his jersey to examine the little thing. They both stroked her soft fur.

Reuben then noticed the tiny creature was deformed.

"Aww. She was born without a front leg," said Reuben softly.

"Looks like the other one is bent backward," added Jon.

Growing up in a household with dogs, Reuben had learned that mother dogs sometimes suffocate their disabled or weaker offspring, instinctively sensing it's the merciful thing to do.

> From under the boy's shirt, the little doggie, still shivering, coils into a fur ball. But it's warmer there than out in the cold winter air. Then, as the boy begins to walk, the movement makes her sleepy.

"Mom! Jon's dog had her litter. She was mean, growling like the dickens . . . sitting on the head of one of the babies, trying to kill it."

Jude noticed a little movement under Reuben's jersey and looked askance, as if to say, *I thought I told you . . .*

Quickly pleading his case, Reuben lifted the jersey, handing her the tiny puppy. "Mom, she needs us. If I didn't save her, she'd be dead."

Holding that little clump of fur, Jude couldn't get mad at her son. Bringing home a wounded creature was exactly what she would have done under the same circumstances.

"Do you think she'll survive, Mom? She's so cute."

Jude was doubtful. The poor thing was odd looking . . . born with so many strikes against her.

"Well . . . let's see what the vet says about this puppy to-morrow," said Jude softly, trying to remain noncommittal.

At that moment Caity walked into the kitchen, saw that her mother was holding something, overheard the word "puppy," turned, and dashed down the hall to tell her sister. "Laura. Laura! Mom's got a new puppy!"

🐾   🐾   🐾

The next morning Jude handed the little pup to her friend Dr. Diane Delbridge, whom she'd known since third grade.

She'd often joked, "You really know your vet if you've climbed the monkey bars together."

Diane concluded that the puppy's hind legs were perfectly normal but cautioned that the deformed left front leg would have to be watched carefully.

"Assuming this little dog lives, she won't have an easy life. She can't scoot on the ground without injuring her chest. And the nonfunctional front leg will be an impediment, just getting in the way."

As she spoke, the doctor was thinking out loud. "We need to come up with a way for her to be more upright. Maybe an apparatus that straps onto the dog, with wheels carrying the front part of her body."

When she finished advising Jude on how and what to feed the puppy, Diane looked at Jude, not as a patient, but as an old friend: "This dog doesn't need to die," she said. "But if she lives, it'll be due to the loving care she receives from you and your family."

Over the next several weeks Jude and the kids pulled together as a family, taking turns caring for the pup. Each of the kids took on a task in return for being able to sleep with her for part of the night, as prescribed by a punctual schedule drawn up by Reuben. As the oldest child, and the only boy, he had taken on the mantle of "man of the house."

The girls took turns bathing the pup that Jude started calling Yellow Dog, and everyone participated in feeding her, first with Tiger's Milk on a Q-tip . . . then from a teaspoon . . . and eventually helping her to drink from a bowl.

🐾 🐾 🐾

Weeks later, following the vet's suggestion that perhaps some kind of cart could be made to hold up her front torso, Jude and the kids got to work. Reuben stripped some wheels off a toy Tonka truck and they built an apparatus attached by a harness.

But Yellow Dog would have none of it. She was already beginning to show the world that, despite her disability, she was going to be an alpha dog. The leader of the pack.

One day when Yellow Dog was about three months old, Reuben left her sleeping on the couch and went into the kitchen. As he was about to open the refrigerator, he stepped on something soft. It was Yellow Dog, somehow underfoot. For the first time the pup made a noise!

"Oh no, I'm so sorry—are you okay?" He picked her up, hugging and kissing her.

"Mom, Yellow Dog got off the couch all by herself," he said as Jude walked into the kitchen.

"Maybe we should find a better place for her to rest," observed Jude. "We don't want her falling and breaking her neck."*

It was a nice day with light snow on the ground, and Reuben had another big idea. "I'm taking her outside to teach her how to sit up," he said, not quite clarifying how learning to sit up would keep the pup from falling off the couch. Opening the door, Reuben let out the other family dogs as well: Matrix, a dachshund beagle mix, and Ean, a short, stocky corgi.

Reuben began his training. He'd prop the dog up, watch her fall over in the snow, then repeat the process. The toy she held in her mouth fell to the ground.

Ean decided to get in on the action. He stuck his nose in between Reuben and Yellow Dog, nipped her, and took off across the yard with her toy.

> *Ouch!* Somewhere, deep in her spirit, Yellow Dog has already determined that she *is* going to survive and she *isn't* going to be pushed around, especially by a corgi!

---

* Jude Stringfellow, *Faith Walks: A Memoir of a Beautiful Life* (iUniverse), Kindle Edition, 551.

In one graceful move, she plopped forward, pushed up from the ground with her chin, and managed to rise up on her two hind legs. As Reuben watched in astonishment, his puppy took on the look of a toddler just learning to walk, putting one foot in front of the other, then walking a little more rapidly . . . then actually chasing Ean. The other dog seemed unsure if this was a game or if he was running for his life from a dog walking like a human.

"You should have seen Ean take off," said Reuben later as everyone gathered for supper and the family excitedly talked about the amazing turn of events. Their little puppy was now doing what seemed to be the impossible: walking—and running—on two legs, capable of literally standing above her peers.

Reuben raised a question they'd avoided for a long time; the newest member of the family needed a proper name.

"I like what I've been calling her," said Jude.

"Yellow Dog isn't a name," one of the girls chimed in, "it's a description."

"She's not really yellow," said the other one.

"More the color of peanut butter," said the first.

"Because she survived, I think her name should be Angel," said Caity.

"What about you, Reuben?" asked Jude.

Squinching his face in thought, Reuben spoke with

mock seriousness. "My choice is 'Doggie' . . . but pronounced, like in French, 'DOH-gee.'"

Everyone let that one go.

Laura was introspective. "I think we should call her 'Faith.' Because if she can make it . . . walking on her own . . . it's because she has faith in herself."

Everyone was quiet for a moment. They knew she was right. *That* was the very best name of all.

"Faith! You have a new name," said Reuben to his little puppy, stroking her head.

Faith looks up, wondering what all the commotion is about. *What's everyone looking at? Why are they saying that word, over and over?* She doesn't know, but she loves the attention.

Faith's ability to stand and walk upright fostered another big idea from Reuben. He would get her in shape by teaching her some of the drills he'd learned in high school football. Again, putting together a punctual schedule, the boy and his dog began a daily regimen of squats . . . first Reuben, then Faith. Then they'd do their sprints. First Reuben would run around the dining room table, then Faith would mimic him.

When Dr. Delbridge gave Faith her six-month checkup, she was astonished to see the pup walking on two legs. She concluded that Faith's hind legs were strong and developing in a healthy manner. She could stand about three-quarters upright, which was the right balance for her. The vet also determined that Faith had no feeling in her disabled left front leg and that it was more of a hindrance than a help. With the consent of Jude and the family, the useless left front leg was removed.

Faith had a small bandage for a couple days, but gave no indication of pain.

By learning to walk like a human, Faith had become the uncontested alpha dog in the Stringfellow household. On two legs, she stood over and dominated Matrix and Ean, as well as the other rescue dogs that were occasionally fostered there. And no creature had the guts to touch Faith's food.

One Friday, Faith had no idea that her life was about to change forever. For several weeks Jude had left messages at several Oklahoma City newspapers and TV stations telling them about a unique story of hope . . . about a little dog that wouldn't give up. No one called back. But on that day, she received a call from KFOR. Saying it was a slow news day, the producer asked about a dog that presumably could walk on two legs.

> When the men in the truck come into the house,
> Faith is delighted to be the center of attention. The

men hold black boxes called *cameras* up to their
faces and keep laughing as she walks around for
them.

Later, when Jude and the kids are gathered around
the TV in the living room, they all begin squealing
just as Faith sees herself strutting across the screen.
She doesn't know what the big deal is, but she's glad
everybody is so happy.

All it took was for one local TV station to pass the story
on to the Associated Press, which shares stories with news
outlets around the globe, and the phone started ringing like
crazy.

Other TV programs, newspapers, and radio stations
wanted to come see Faith the walking dog. Then a big call
came in: the *Ripley's Believe It or Not!* show producers asked
if they could send a crew to produce a segment for the television series hosted by Dean Cain.

For the next three years, dozens more shows followed:
Inside Edition, Animal Planet programs, and then the most
special call of all came from the *Oprah Winfrey Show* in
Chicago.

The producers spoke with Jude several times, reminding
her that she was sworn to secrecy because they wanted to
surprise Oprah on the day of the show. Jude and Laura were

originally going to fly to Harpo Studios in Chicago, but at the last minute Jude wasn't feeling well, so instead, she sent Laura and Caity, now seventeen and sixteen.

Faith had become a ham, loving the attention of live audiences. Filled with anticipation, Laura and Faith stood behind sliding doors that looked like the back of a movie screen. They heard the voice of Oprah setting up the show segment.

> In the dim backstage light, Faith gets more and more excited by the loud cheering sounds of people who seem to laugh and clap at everything the woman who is talking has to say.

"My producers told me that I was going to love this next segment," said Oprah, beginning her introduction. "I have not met our next guest, but my staff tells me that I'll never forget this girl . . . she's a one-of-a-kind miracle . . . and the fact that she can walk out on this stage today is beyond all reason. Fittingly, her name is 'Faith.' So, come on out, Faith!"

> Faith watches as the screen parts in the middle. She can suddenly smell hundreds of different people scents all at once! As she hops and then walks rapidly toward the lady, Faith looks into a sea of

smiling, joyful faces. The lady's mouth is wide open.
She keeps saying, "I have never . . . I have never . . .
I have never."

Faith walked right up to Oprah as she exclaimed, "Oh
my God . . . it's a two-legged dog!"

Oprah Winfrey's show elevated Faith's celebrity to a new
level. She was recognized everywhere she went. At airports
and public places, people always wanted to have pictures
taken with her.

Faith loved the growing crowds and the attention as
they traveled around the country. One day she was standing next to Jude in a hotel lobby. Jude was preoccupied,
talking to some people, when Faith heard applause from a
nearby room.

What's that? The applause is Faith's cue. She rapidly
follows the clapping sound right into an adjacent
hotel ballroom.

She walks down a long aisle, lined with people
who are standing up looking at her and smiling . . .
She is following right behind a man in a tuxedo
who is escorting a lady wearing a white lacy dress,
part of it dragging on the floor. People first look
at the lady, then at Faith, breaking into laughter
and clapping.

Jude looked down. Faith was gone! When she heard raucous laughter and applause, she knew exactly where to find her dog. Running into the ballroom, Jude was horrified. Faith had crashed a wedding!

Only later did everyone agree that Faith's impromptu actions had made the bride's special day more memorable than she could have imagined. Not to mention sending it viral on the internet.

Jude was convinced that Faith was more than an accident that Reuben had once brought home and convinced his mom to keep. Faith had been divinely aligned to be discovered by her son on that cold day behind the fence. This dog had a job for God, and she was performing it every time she demonstrated her power of perseverance.

That was never more apparent than the day Jude and Faith were invited to visit the Walter Reed Army Medical Center in the nation's capital.

C'mon, Jude . . . you can't cry now, she told herself, pressing her lips together as they approached the entrance to the mammoth hospital for wounded warriors in northeast Washington, DC. *You've got soldiers to see . . . hold it together!*

She could not escape the fact that her own son was now a soldier. Yes, the teenaged boy named Reuben who had once had the heart to rescue a baby puppy from suffocation, then help it to walk on two legs, was now serving his country overseas.

This was a moment that called for prayer.

Jude had become highly experienced in praying for her son and his fellow warriors. It had also crossed her mind that the mothers of soldiers, sailors, and airmen probably said more prayers more times every day than the rest of the population, always asking for God's assistance in keeping their children safe.

Now, Jude and Faith were about to come face-to-face with soldiers who had been broken and battered by war, many missing arms or legs, just like her little dog.

"It was very moving. I could not believe the carnage I was seeing," she later recalled. "I wanted to throw my arms around the neck of every combatant, thank them for their service, and call their mothers to cry with them."

What was amazing was how nearly every one of these courageous soldiers couldn't wait to return to their units to carry on with their mission.*

Of all the soldiers they encountered that first day, Jude was particularly taken with Frankie. Jude and Faith spotted Frankie being wheeled from surgery to his recovery room; he was still sedated.

---

* Ibid.: Kindle location 1153 & 1154.

Faith first notices the strong smell of antiseptic
medicine as the gurney comes down the corridor
toward her. She isn't sure why, but she feels
something for this young man. She begins
to whimper.

Frankie looked down, groggy, and mumbled, "Come
here, dog."

Faith cocked her head.

"Get up here right now," he commanded.

She leaps, landing next to Frankie. She now can
see what they have in common. They've both
lost legs. She showers him in kisses, letting
him know how she feels. That seems to make
him happy.

"Something told me," said Jude, "that the smiles on
the faces and the tears in the eyes of those soldiers when
they met Faith were the real reason she was allowed to
live."*

---

* Ibid.: Kindle location 1200.

Reflections

Faith the walking dog lived a full life of twelve years.

There is no way to calculate the number of people whose spirits were lifted by this gritty little dog who stood as tall as a child, but had a giant-sized hunger for survival and an innate desire to encourage others who faced similar challenges.

Whenever Jude brought out Faith's little ACU jacket, the dog was never happier. The Army Combat Uniform had been given to her at Fort Lewis, along with her non-commission rank of E-5 Sergeant.*

When Faith visited military hospitals throughout the world, her spunk and determination warmed the hearts and triggered the tears of more than two thousand wounded warriors. Additionally, she was seen by more than two million active soldiers at events and ceremonies. Add to that the vast audiences of people whose spirits were lifted by seeing Faith walk across the screen on scores of national television programs.

Jude Stringfellow and her kids were glad to be right

---

* "Faith (dog)," Wikipedia, https://en.wikipedia.org/wiki/Faith_(dog), accessed January 16, 2020.

alongside Faith for her entire earthly journey of bringing hope to others, especially soldiers. Their own faith was always strengthened by the yellow dog's faith in herself. Often Jude would remind herself: "God made this unique dog; He will help me to help her."* But she wonders, *How often was it the other way around, with Faith helping me?*

That pup fulfilled God's purpose in Jude's life: to teach all of us to never give up, no matter what. If we persevere, we can be victorious . . . if we just have faith.

---

* Ibid.: Kindle location 439.

17

SIERRA

Preparing a pot of coffee and getting the bacon and eggs sizzling on the stove, Stephanie Herfel, forty-eight years old, furrowed her brow as she looked out her kitchen window at the beautiful San Diego sunrise peeking over the horizon.

What am I getting myself into? she thought as she set out a second coffee cup, a plate, and silverware.

My life is comfortable. I'm used to living alone. I have a nice little business right here at home, and I don't even have to fight traffic getting to work. I like my life! This feels like a big complication.

She heard a car door slam. Her son was arriving, just as he'd said on the phone. She again glanced out the window.

Oh my goodness. He's bigger than I thought!

She was watching as Sean, dressed in military camo,

came up the walk holding a leash connected to a large dog—a black-and-white husky.

Sierra is so glad to finally jump out of the car and into the crisp morning air. The drive was long— twenty-four hours—with not many stops.

Sean kept saying, "Sorry, Sierra, I have to get you there and get myself back."

Now she is tugging on the leash, letting Sean know she'd like to stop for a moment . . . for dog business.

Sierra didn't know what Sean meant when he said, *I'm being deployed and you're staying with Mom.* Human language was sometimes hard to figure out.

But she liked the tone in his voice when he told her, *You're going to like it there a lot.*

Stephanie hugged her son, looked down at the husky, almost as tall as the kitchen table, and said, "She's so beautiful . . . and . . . so big."

"Sorry, Mom, I know you've got tight quarters here, but I didn't have a choice. My friend John promised to take Sierra, then, at the last minute, said he had a change of plans, couldn't take her. If he did, he'd end up selling her. Mom, that would break my heart."

She put her hand gently on her son's face and softly said, "We'll make it work."

She turned, grabbed the coffeepot, and smiled. "You're just in time for bacon and eggs. Sit down, honey."

> Following Sean's lead, Sierra lies on the floor next to his chair.
>
> Just as the husky expected, Sean reaches down and strokes her neck.
>
> She sniffs. *This might be a very nice place to live. That bacon sure smells good.*
>
> Just then, Sean drops her a strip of bacon. *Yep. Tastes good too.*

An hour later Sean had gobbled down his breakfast, said his goodbyes, and started back to Shreveport for deployment two days later.

For the umpteenth time, the thought crossed Stephanie's mind: *What am I getting myself into?*

Her misgivings were understandable. She already had a large dog, Nana. So taking on a second oversized furry roommate, in a small but stylish single-family home, raised reasonable worries.

But her trepidation was short-lived. Sierra turned out to be a remarkably comforting companion.

Of course Sierra misses Sean, but she has no
trouble adopting Stephanie as her new best friend.

It's fun to go on walks together; she likes remaining
close to Stephanie as she does her work—there is
never a moment that she doesn't feel loved.

Sure, there is that other dog, Nana. They get
along. But Sierra is convinced that she is Stephanie's
favorite.

One year later, Stephanie was on the phone with her
aunt and uncle who lived in Madison, Wisconsin. They
were getting older and she felt a strong inner nudge to
move there so she could be of help to them.

"No, it wouldn't be a bother," she told her aunt. "My
work is at home, so I can live anywhere. I just think it's
time that Sierra, Nana, and I moved to the Midwest to be
close to you."

Weeks later Sierra finds herself adapting to another
location. And a different home.

She enjoys their frequent visits with Stephanie's
aunt and uncle, and during walks with Stephanie
in the new city she can feel the cooler fall
temperatures, and for the first time she smells
dry leaves and bonfires.

*As far as Sierra is concerned, where they live
doesn't matter; home is wherever Stephanie is.*

During the early part of the following year Stephanie
was experiencing an unexpected weight gain and had a
redundant pain in her abdomen. She finally went to the
emergency room.

A CAT scan suggested that she had an ovarian cyst.
Doctors gave her pain medication and recommended
watching and waiting. Yet all summer long, and into the
early fall, she just wasn't improving and no one seemed to
be able to help her. It turned out she'd been given a terrible
misdiagnosis.

🐾   🐾   🐾

As Stephanie was sitting in a chair reading a book one day,
Sierra was hanging closer to her than usual. The husky
pressed her nose into Stephanie's belly in a manner that
created discomfort. It was highly uncharacteristic of her
dog. Stephanie gently pushed Sierra away, but she repeated
the action.

"Sierra, stop!" Stephanie finally snapped. The dog walked
away.

Sierra feels scolded by Stephanie's tone of voice. She's never been spoken to in a cross manner.

All she was trying to do was tell Stephanie something . . . but she doesn't know how. If only she could use words the way humans do.

With hurt feelings, Sierra senses that maybe she needs to separate herself from Stephanie for a while.

Some fifteen or twenty minutes passed before Stephanie realized that her best friend was no longer at her side.

"Sierra?" she called. She pulled herself from the chair and went to the kitchen. Then the bedroom. "Sierra?" she called again and again.

She checked the front door to make sure her husky hadn't gotten out. It was closed. "Sierra!" she called louder.

It was inexplicable. Her dog was always obedient and had never just disappeared. Stephanie retraced her steps through every room, even looking in the bathtub and closets.

"Sierra, where are you?!" She began to cry.

Once more she looked everywhere, under the bed, in the closets, and was about to close a closet door when she saw something black and white peeking from under a low-hanging rack of blouses that nearly touched floor level. It was the tip of a tail.

On her knees, Stephanie parted the blouses. "Sierra?" she said softly, suddenly feeling her heart sink, shocked by the saddest expression she'd ever witnessed on her sweet dog's face.

The fur all around Sierra's eyes was damp.

Stephanie had never heard of a dog crying tears—but, could this be described in any other way?

Pushing the blouses further aside, Stephanie crawled in to be with her dear friend, to hug her, and to tell her she was sorry for speaking harshly.

Slowly she stood up and invited Sierra to come with her . . . for her dinner.

A while later as she watched Sierra and Nana, side by side, at their twin dog bowls, Stephanie couldn't help wondering.

Could Sierra have been trying to tell me something? Something that the doctors couldn't find? But maybe she could, through extraordinary canine senses?

The next day Stephanie arranged an appointment with her doctor and explained what had happened.

"I think Sierra was pressing her nose to my tummy to tell me something," she told the doctor, "and when I didn't listen, she hid to get my attention."

Stephanie took another battery of tests and this time the news was definitive and devastating. Her doctor tried to be as gentle as possible, but hearing that you have stage-three ovarian cancer is like getting hit with a sledge hammer. They call it the "silent killer" because people often do not have symptoms until it's too late.* But, thanks to Sierra, the doctor said it was discovered in time to give her a chance for survival.

Stephanie had surgery and the cancer was removed.

The doctor was so impressed with Sierra's early detection that he did his own research, sharing his discoveries with Stephanie:

"Dogs have smell receptors 10,000 times more accurate than humans, making them highly sensitive to odors we can't perceive," he reported, and added that "a new study has shown that dogs can use their highly evolved sense of smell to pick out blood samples from people with cancer with almost 97 percent accuracy."†

Sierra was one of those dogs who could smell cancer even before the doctor's tests could confirm it. Four more times, over the next five years, she detected the odd scent, somehow knowing it was not good for Stephanie and that

---

* https://www.today.com/health/woman-says-dog-saved-her-life-smelled-ovarian-cancer-4-t168047, accessed December 17, 2019.

† "Study shows dogs can accurately sniff out cancer in blood," *Science Daily*, April 8, 2019, https://www.sciencedaily.com/releases/2019/04/190408114304.htm.

she had to let her know. She never again pressed her nose against Stephanie to get her attention. That didn't work well. But hiding was how she learned to communicate with Stephanie, sending her an early warning that something was wrong.

She repeated her pattern of hiding in the closet and one time under the bed. On another occasion they were visiting someone's house. There was no closet or bed she could get access to, so she went into the bathroom and curled up behind the commode.

As scary as it was for Stephanie to repeatedly learn that her cancer had returned, it was reassuring to know that she had a very special God-given advance scout who was ferreting out trouble, sometimes months before medical tests could confirm her detection.

With Sierra in charge of comfort, Stephanie was able to keep things in perspective and find the joy in every day. She even met a wonderful man named Jim—they fell in love and were married, but not before Stephanie gave him the chance to leave the relationship when the cancer returned.

Jim said, "I love you, Stephanie. I don't care what you have. We'll get through everything together."

And they have.

Sierra knew she liked that man Jim. He's very kind.

And he helps her take care of Stephanie.

Reflections

The divine alignment of Godwinks happens in everyone's life; we find ourselves at the right place at the right time for God's will to unfold.

Stephanie wasn't looking for another large furry roommate, but Sierra was divinely aligned into her life, by her son's deployment, to reveal a life-threatening medical issue that even modern medicine couldn't detect.

It appears that God's army of angels on earth includes pets like Sierra, who are engaged to deliver Godwink dogwinks.

"Welcome strangers into your home . . . some people have welcomed angels as guests, without even knowing it."
—HEBREWS 13:2[*]

---

[*] Contemporary English Version.

18

BOOGA

"Hold on, Mac . . . I'm not going to leave you!" shouted Gerry, the younger of the two men struggling to keep their heads above water.

"I'm cold . . . I don't think I can hold on any longer," said Mac, his body shivering, his lips blue from the cold December waters.

"Just keep hanging on to that stick!" shouted Gerry, trying desperately to believe his own words. "It'll be light soon . . . somebody'll see us."

Booga, a black Labrador retriever, is swimming in circles, as best he can, in the cold, heaving waters. Moments before, he had been in the boat with Mac and his friend Gerry. The winds suddenly changed

and the waves rose above the sides of the boat,
smashing the small vessel up and down. Next thing
he knew, Booga was underwater!

He struggled to the surface, and in between
waves he could see the two men. They were
trying to hold on to a pole sticking up from the
water.

Gerry Ponson, his friend Mac Ansespy, and his dog, Booga, had left shore at 5 in the morning. Their mission: to cross the three-mile bay near New Orleans to their favorite duck-hunting spot. The forecast had called for nasty weather, but Gerry said if they got their seventeen-foot open-bay boat across early enough, they could make it. But just before they reached the spot in the bay where Gerry knew there was a deep drop-off—the channel—the waters quickly became choppy as a northwester charged toward them, tossing their craft up and down like a toy.

The seawater splashed over them and the rough waters seized the direction of the boat, causing it to turn sideways to the waves. Mac was steering.

"Turn the boat, turn the boat!" Gerry shouted, but it was too late. A huge wave crashed in on them, instantly filling their boat, causing it to sink in eight feet of water.

One of the few items in the craft that Gerry could grab

was a ten-foot push pole used for pushing a boat through shallow waters. By plunging the stick into the mud and standing on the sunken vessel's gunnels, they could just keep their heads above water.

"Grab that pole, Mac, and hold on," Gerry repeated to his friend.

> Booga is getting tired. It is difficult to stay afloat. The waves are tossing him this way and that. It's like he's in a washing machine that keeps flinging him a distance away and he has to keep swimming back, against the current, to get to where the men are.
>
> Thank goodness, every once in a while Gerry grabs his collar, says some reassuring words, and holds him up, while hanging on to the pole with his other hand.

Gerry assessed their situation. He knew Mac was in no shape to swim to shore. Besides, until the sun came up, they might be swimming in circles. He also considered leaving Mac and Booga, swimming for help. But even if he made it ashore, it was five miles to the nearest phone. And Mac couldn't survive on his own. No . . . he'd wait . . . maybe a boat would come up the channel.

As he'd done for two hours, Gerry propped up Mac,

then grabbed the dog by the collar and helped him stay afloat for a few minutes. Finally, Gerry had to make a difficult decision. He told Booga to go.

> Booga is smart. A national champion retriever. He knows what Gerry is saying, but . . . *Does he really mean it when he says . . . "git"?*
>
> He hears it again. "Git, Booga, git!"
>
> Booga follows the command. His job is to find his way to land. If he can.
>
> *Smash* . . . Another big wave picks him up; he is topsy-turvy. Pulled under.

"Where's Booga?" gasped Mac, disoriented after all that time in the cold waters, looking around for his black Lab.

"I tol' him to git. I can save you, Mac, but I can't save your dog."

In his heart he knew the dog would never make it. A mile back to shore in those nasty waters would be too much for any creature.

Gerry's constant movement was staving off hypothermia, but Mac's body temperature plunged dangerously low, starting to cause a shutdown of bodily functions in the frigid waters and biting wind.

"I'm cold, Gerry . . . I can't hold on any longer," Mac panted, mentally beginning to let go.

"Hold on, Mac. Somebody'll come."

Gerry didn't really believe that.

He didn't believe in anything. He'd been a heathen all his adult life. There were times as a kid when he sort of allowed that God existed, but as an adult he was a self-described "drinkin', cheatin' heathen, looking for love in all the wrong places."

His sister had tried. She tried to talk to him about God, but he'd called her a fruitcake—and worse—told her to "get her *blankety-blank* outta his house."

Smash!

A wave drenched him.

"Hold on, Mac!"

Booga surfaces, struggling to maintain a sense of where he is heading. There is nothing but water. No land. No boat in sight. He only has a sense, a deep inner sense, to keep swimming in one particular direction.

Smash. Every wave is his enemy. Trying to pull him under, rob him of air.

Maybe Gerry should have listened to her. His sister. His girlfriend too. Shannon was also one of those "believers." She gave him less hassle, though. Didn't press him like his sister . . . gave him his space. But he knew, underneath, without even saying so, she also wanted him to come on board with God. He missed her. *I hope I get to see her again*, he thought.

"I can't hold on anymore," said Mac, weaker now.

Smash. Another wave. But . . . now, at least, three hours into their ordeal, the winds seemed to be settling down a bit.

"Yes, you can! Hold on," encouraged Gerry, trying to buy his own baloney, but this was bad. Really bad. Inside his head he was saying, *We're gonna die out here. Nobody's comin' . . . we're gonna die.*

Gerry lifted his eyes toward the sky, unsure of how to say what he was going to say.

"God . . . if you hear me . . . please, give me a second chance. Send us a boat. Please save us . . ." Then, screaming in desperation, "PLEASE . . . A SECOND CHANCE, GOD!"

His own words startled him . . . He couldn't believe what he had just said. If there was a God, why in the world would He think Gerry deserved a second chance?

But—not two minutes later—he couldn't believe what his eyes were seeing.

"Mac . . . I see something!"

Through the morning mist Gerry could see the shadows of a cross. *What? No, wait*—it was the mast of a boat coming down the channel. Through the haze he started to make it out . . . a big boat . . . probably seventy-five feet long.

"It's a boat, Mac, they'll see us. Hold on to me!" he shouted, pulling the push pole from the mud, attaching his shirt to one end, waving it frantically in the air.

"Over here!" he shouted repeatedly.

Doubtful thoughts rushed into his mind. *Who would see us—just blobs in rough waters?*

"Make 'em see us, God!" shouted Gerry, now in for a penny, in for a pound.

"Mac . . . I think they see us! They've stopped! But that big boat can't get over here. It's not deep enough."

Then Gerry saw someone coming toward them. In an inflatable motorboat.

"They're coming, Mac, hold on!"

A man pulled Mac into the boat, then helped Gerry in.

As the boat splashed its way to the big boat, Gerry began to realize what had just happened. Within moments of asking for help from the Almighty, the one boat that had come up that channel that morning actually saw them, and saved them! This was too much to grasp.

Moments later, Mac was hoisted up in a huge basket and the man asked Gerry if he could climb the rope ladder. He said he could.

But as Gerry climbed toward the deck, he saw the name on the side of the boat. It struck him—like a bolt of lightning. He knew right then and there that God had heard his pleading prayer and had definitely saved him.

The name of the boat was *Second Chance.*

He shook his head. His eyes watered up. He knew, from that moment on, his life would never be the same.

The Coast Guard sent a helicopter, hoisting Mac upward as Gerry shouted, "I'll come to the hospital as soon as I can, Mac."

A half hour later Gerry was let out on a dock in New Orleans. It felt good to be back on land. He'd thought about the conversations he was going to have with Shannon. And his sister.

He was still pinching himself. Still not believing that he wasn't in some kind of dream, in which God had reached down and saved a heathen like him.

Woof.

"Booga? Is that you?"

The two ran toward each other, joyfully hugging!

Booga had kept on swimming until he smelled the fishing boats in New Orleans Harbor. That was his beacon to swim the distance, finally pulling himself onto shore, finding his way to a marshy area near a dock.

Spotting water in a rain trough, he took a few licks before spreading himself on the grass, closing his eyes.

Then he smelled him. It was Gerry!

Tears welled in Gerry's eyes again. He couldn't believe that God was offering second chances all around!

"I don't believe it, Booga! Mac and me both got second chances today . . . and so did you!"

Booga wags his tail. Whatever exhaustion he'd been feeling after all that swimming is now gone. He is full of energy. His friend Gerry is here!

And his ears perk up when Gerry says, "Let's go see Mac, Booga! He is going to be so happy to see you!"

Booga jumps up and down as if to say, *What are we waiting for?*

Reflections

Mac was released from the hospital two days later. He and Booga were able to travel to the next dog show competition.

Booga used his second chance to once again come home as a blue-ribbon champion!

Gerry Ponson had unquestionably experienced a major transformation in his life. It was forever emblazoned on his heart what had happened to him just as he was giving up all hope. He shouted out a prayer to someone to whom he'd never spoken. He asked for a second chance. And the prayer was instantly answered. A boat named *Second Chance* showed up.

Gerry was determined to make things right with his sister. And as for Shannon? He asked her to marry him. She was thrilled that her man had a new heart. They were wed two weeks later.

For years now, Gerry has been a street preacher, working with Celebration Church in New Orleans.

He tells folks he encounters on the streets that God can do anything. "You just need to pray, fervently, regardless of how rough the waters are," he says, telling them his amazing story. Then he shares something that the captain of the *Second Chance* ship told him. That boat wasn't even supposed to be there that morning. The storm altered the tides, causing that big boat to take the channel instead of their normal route via the Gulf of Mexico.

Love those Godwinks. And dogwinks.

19

BOGART

"Mama," said the little boy, wide-eyed, "he's just like me!"

Landon, a cute, blond, four-year-old boy, was holding a tiny puppy. He couldn't believe the happiness he was feeling as he looked into the pup's face. The little dog had the same birth defect that Landon himself had been struggling with all his life . . . a cleft lip and cleft palate.

> The little pup reaches up and licks the soft face of the boy whose heart is beating with excitement under his jammies. There is something special about him.

The child's mother, Kelly Sayer, could hardly contain her joy. Her son had endured so much and now he was bubbling over like a shaken-up soda bottle! This was a major Godwink!

During recent months the little boy had become progressively withdrawn and depressed. He had been noticing that kids were staring at him, that he was different. It was the time Kelly had always dreaded . . . when her son would become the object of ridicule over something he couldn't control; something that wasn't his fault.

But this was a moment to savor! The kind of joy that comes along only a handful of times when everything connects for a perfect outcome. That's when you know God has had a hand in it.

Since her own childhood, Kelly had been a dog lover. She volunteered at animal shelters as a teenager, prompting her field of study as a veterinarian technician. And, right up until the time she learned that Landon would be born with special needs, she couldn't remember a time when she wasn't fostering dogs awaiting adoptive homes.

When she saw her son withdrawing, she felt that a puppy friend might be just what he needed.

What a Godwink when she arrived at the animal rescue and discovered they had just taken in a newborn puppy with a cleft lip, on the same side as Landon's!

It was like a gift from above, she said. "A little puppy

angel who came into my son's life just when he needed him."

"What's his name, Mama?" asked Landon, rubbing his cheek against the soft fur of the little pup.

Kelly beamed again as the furry creature wiggled playfully with Landon. "The animal rescue called him Bogart. Do you like that name?"

Landon nodded, then looked up at his mother expectantly. "Can I keep him, Mama? Can we keep Bogart?"

"Yes. Bogart is special, just like you. And he's your new friend."

"I just love him, Mama," said the little towhead, hugging his new puppy, whose patches of fur had the same blondish coloring as Landon's own hair.

🐾 🐾 🐾

Caring for Bogart was, in its own way, almost as challenging for Kelly as tending to Landon as an infant. The puppy didn't have the capacity to swallow easily and therefore couldn't eat or drink normally. He had to be tube-fed every two hours.

Kelly engaged Landon in the process. Whenever she wasn't feeding Bogart, Landon was holding and comforting him. They developed a special bond.

As the small mixed-breed mutt grew, he loved to scamper on the hardwood floors, usually with Landon right behind.

> Bogart loves scooting around the house, skidding around corners, and rushing back to his new boy for hugs and kisses!

One day Kelly had a big idea. "Do you think Bogart would like a ride on the Roomba?" She giggled at the very thought of it.

"Really, Mama?" Landon grinned.

"Bogart loves it, Mama!" Landon laughed as he watched his new puppy riding the circular floor cleaner like a ride at the carnival.

> Wheeeeeee! Bogart knew he was really going to like this place and this new boy!

"I love you, Bogart," said Landon, gathering up the wiggly furry pup in his arms. "You're my special friend."

> Bogart can't understand the words, but he gets the message. Delivered through little-boy kisses. So, he does what dogs do. He kisses him back!

Reflections

It is estimated that 1 in 700 children are born with cleft lips or palates.* Though a similar statistic for puppies has not been found, Kelly Sayer will tell you that it's more common than you might think. But the challenge for puppies born with clefts is difficulty in nursing and aspirating, often causing pneumonia or starvation.

Kelly says that Bogart brings out the best in Landon, helping him to put his own challenges into perspective. He sees that even puppies can be born with challenges, yet can still lead happy lives.

Because of their bond and connection, Kelly says that Landon has a sense of peace that he didn't have before.

Bogart is very intuitive to Landon's feelings. When he's sad, Bogart knows how to comfort him.

Landon, who wants to be a veterinarian when he grows up, has become an ambassador for Operation Smile, a charitable organization that provides surgery to repair cleft lips and cleft palates. Their mission is to help bring new smiles to children around the world.

---

* Smile Train Charity, https://www.smiletrain.org/our-cause/what-is-cleft.

20

MUFF

"Harley had her litter, Mom!" Amy excitedly greets her mother, who is coming through the kitchen door. "Twelve of the cutest Dalmatians you've ever seen!"

Amy Collins and her mom live a half hour apart east of Oklahoma City. Amy is in Midwest City and Donna in Harrah.

"Come look!" she says, heading for the laundry room, a temporary fenced-in nursery. "One is so darling, so unique, she has solid brown spots covering her ears." She adds with a giggle, "John says she looks like she's wearing earmuffs! So, I called her Muff . . . and we're going to keep her."

"Oh, that's nice, honey," Donna says, stroking the wiggly little pup that Amy plops into her arms. "A sweet companion for your own babies." She looks at her daughter with a trace of concern. "How're you feeling?"

"Pretty good," says Amy, touching her rounded belly. "The twins are starting to rock and roll in there!"

"How's our other mother doing this morning?" Donna asks, looking at Harley.

"She's as pooped as I am. But at least . . . *she* delivered!"

Dozing on and off, Harley lies on her dog mat that Amy and John placed in a corner of the laundry room. Giving birth to twelve squirming puppies was a lot of work! But now . . . she can finally rest . . . if only these puppies would stop demanding attention.

Muff enjoyed the adoration she was getting from Amy and Donna. She has no idea what is in store for her; that once her brothers and sisters have been put up for adoption in ten weeks, she'll have the family, and her mom, all to herself!

Muff responds to the petting with little whimpering sounds while licking Amy and Donna, letting them know she likes it.

One Year Later—3 p.m.

Muff is now a fully formed young dog. She has the energy and excitability of all Dalmatians, and her whiteness as a newborn has been replaced with brown spots all over her body. Her telltale "earmuffs" make her look like a Dalmatian puppy right out of a Disney movie.

> Muff romps through the house, following her nose and the wonderful scent of babies—like vanilla cookies—looking for her best friends.
>
> *There they are! There they are!* Amy has the girls, Emerson and Preslee, up on the bed.
>
> Taking a good leap, Muff jumps up, and excitedly nuzzles the four-month-old twins. They respond happily as always. She licks their hands, savoring their taste and that delicious baby scent.

Amy's not in the mood for frivolity this afternoon; she's in a hurry. "Muff, get down. We're getting dressed here."

Instantly aware that her tone of voice might have sounded abrupt and insensitive, Amy remembers that she picked up something she had special-ordered for her dogs online.

"Muff, come here; I have something for you and Harley. You can get dressed too, just like the girls." Muff sits. Amy places a dog collar around her neck. Her name is engraved into the leather, "MUFF."

To show Harley, Muff scampers off.

The phone rings. Amy glances at her cellphone lying on the bed. She presses the speaker button so she can continue dressing the babies.

"Hi, Mom."

"Amy, I'm worried about you and the girls. The TV says there's a strong likelihood of tornadoes this afternoon. I'd feel better if you were here with us—our area is less likely to get hit than yours. What's John doing today?"

"He has a softball game after work, not far from the house. We talked about it. Any of his teammates who want to will come over here to our storm shelter. He'll grab the dogs and keep them down there with him. But, Mom . . . I'm getting the girls ready right now . . . we're coming to you. I'm not taking my four-month-old babies into that spidery cellar. So, I'll be there shortly."

One Hour Later—4 p.m.

With the twins buckled into their car seats, Amy leads Harley and Muff into the fenced-in yard, checks on their food and water, and is confident that John will return in time to bring them in.

As she pulls from the driveway, the skies to the south seem to be darkening.

> Muff runs up to her mom, now wearing her own engraved collar, playfully suggesting they play tag. She starts to dart, then stops. Harley hasn't moved. She seems to be concentrating on something. Muff tries again. Finally, she lures Harley into the game, as her mom romps across the yard with Muff chasing after her.
>
> Muff is now sensing something she's never felt before. It scares her. She nuzzles next to Harley, who harkens as if she's listening to far-off noises. She looks worried. Both dogs notice the rustling in the trees. Rain is intermittent, there are rapid changes in the barometric pressure, and they sniff a difference in the air. They are both feeling jittery.

One Hour Later—5 p.m.

Muff and Harley are whimpering. Their animal
instincts tell them there is danger in the atmosphere.
They repeatedly test the gate. It's firmly latched.
They move around the perimeter of the yard
looking for a way to escape. Every internal indicator
tells them this is fight-or-flight time.

Desperately they try to dig under the fence. They
gnaw at the gate. But there's no way out. Harley
circles to the corner of the toolshed where the wire
fence is attached. She stops. Pushes. Pushes again.
The third time the wire fence gives way, just enough
to provide a narrow opening. She and Muff both
squeeze through . . . and dash off!

John Collins is rounding second base, then makes it to
third, and pauses, awaiting the next actions of the pitcher.
The air feels increasingly humid. He looks south and sees
dark and menacing clouds forming. The startling sound of
tornado sirens from the town of Midwest City suddenly
pierces the air. The first warning.

"Hey, guys . . . maybe we should call this game. Look at
those skies. Tornadoes may be coming soon. My house is

close if anyone wants to join me and my dogs in the storm cellar. I might have a few beers stashed down there."

The men disassemble, some heading to their own homes and a handful of others taking up John's invite.

John calls Amy as he drives. No answer. Then he notices she left him a voice mail: "I'm leaving for Mom's house now. Don't forget to bring in Harley and Muff," she reminds him.

John pulls into the driveway, expecting to see the dogs running around the fenced-in yard. But they're not there! With black clouds now ominously close, John quickly tries calling Amy again, but all the circuits are jammed. "I can't reach Amy," he says to his friends. "Maybe she changed her mind . . . took the dogs with her." He and the others grab some snacks from the kitchen and scramble down to the storm cellar.

Amy, at the same time, is trying to call John. She's distraught . . . wanting to know her husband and dogs are secure. She also needs to tell John that she and her mom have decided it's not safe to stay where they are, and they're going to a shelter.

Quickly they place supplies into Amy's car, driving directly to a nearby elementary school that was built with a storm shelter, clean and comfortable, belowground.

Pulling into the school, Amy laments to Donna, seated

in the back with the babies, that she's worried. "I still can't reach John. All the circuits are busy. I pray he got home and got the dogs into the cellar with him." She suddenly has to speak louder to be heard over the eerie wailing sound of tornado sirens, which only heightens the surreal experience and her feelings of fright.

> Harley and Muff have one plan . . . to move quickly away from the black clouds that have now turned a dark greenish color. The air has the smell of fresh rain. The wind has strangely died down.
>
> They come to an intersection. Police cars are stopped, with red-and-blue flashing lights, as policemen quickly move the traffic. A man standing next to a TV truck has a tremor in his voice as he speaks rapidly into a microphone.

"This is the calm before the storm. The air is so still, and the pressure low, that one can feel the impending doom in the stillness," said the TV reporter.

> Muff whimpers loudly. Harley, worried, looks for a safe place to hide. Harley's instincts are to cross the road, heading to the warehouses on the other side. But the cars and trucks are moving dangerously

fast. The rain has now started pelting against their
coats. Worse, they are being struck by golf ball–
sized hail.

The funnel that has formed southwest of Oklahoma
City can be seen for miles away.

The power is out. Straining to hear a staticky radio sig-
nal in the cellar, John and his pals alternate between listening to the news and telling their own stories by candlelight.
There is a tone of nervousness in their jovial talk. John says,
"You know, when you grow up in tornado country, most of
the time we run for shelter, sit and wait, and nothing happens." He looks at the others, adding, "I hope this is one of
those times."

At the school, there is an air of fear. Following the example of dozens of other families, Amy finds a space against
a cement block wall and she and her mom lay out the blankets and sleeping bags. They have water, snacks, and baby
food for the girls. The people next to them have a radio
tuned to News Radio KTOK, which has the attention of
everyone nearby.

"The largest funnel cloud formed ten miles southwest
of OKC, and is moving on a northeasterly path along the
south side of the city," says an authoritative voice. "It will
begin to rain again as the eye of the tornado passes by . . ."

Suddenly the school lights go out . . . there are a few seconds of pitch black . . . then the dim emergency lights flicker on as the power generator automatically kicks in.

Crouching at the side of the road, drenched in rain, it's hard for Harley and Muff to see anything but headlights. There's a sudden halt in the flow of traffic! Harley bolts. Muff follows, dashing through the stopped cars. *BEEP!* The loud car horns cause the dogs to jump. They're frightened . . . running between different stopped cars. *BEEP BEEP!* Trying to survive, they lose sight of each other as the traffic starts to move and the rain pelts down.

Muff gets to the other side. She's safe. But, where's her mom? Harley is nowhere to be seen!

The rain, mixed with hail, is pounding with more and more wind. She barks and whines. She needs to find shelter. Muff runs through drenching rain . . . passes a warehouse, stops . . . crawls beneath an overhang.

Amy pulls the blanket over the babies, who thankfully are only slightly fussy in their twin-child carrier. The ferocious roar of tornado winds can now be heard, even through the strong walls of the storm-fortified school building. She pulls the baby carrier closer, hugs it to herself while darting worried glances to her mother.

Muff shivers, just inches from the drenching downpour. Her eyes carry fear, but she perks up her ears. It sounds like a freight train is coming right at her, getting closer and closer. She has no way of knowing, but that's what tornadoes sound like.

6:30 p.m.

"You hear that?" asks one of the guys with John. "The tornado is close by!"

"It *does* sound like a freight train!" shouts a man, incredulously, who has never endured a tornado before. "And my ears are popping like crazy."

"That's caused by the rapid changes in atmospheric conditions," says John, more loudly now, talking over the additional sound of objects hitting the house.

Minutes later the freight train sounds like it's rumbling away, the battery-operated radio clears up, and the weatherman declares that a ferocious tornado has just passed a mile from Midwest City, and is heading northeast, toward Harrah.

"God, please keep my family safe in Harrah," says John quietly. He's heard by the others, who raise their eyes from their own silent prayers, remaining respectfully quiet.

With a shaking in his voice, a weatherman says, ". . . the winds in these tornadoes are close to exceeding National Weather Service EF standards . . ." The rest of his statement is wiped out by static.

With the most destructive of the tornadoes heading right toward Harrah, and no way to connect, John is feeling panicked.

Finally, after trying dozens of times, he gets connected. Into the phone John sighs, and he feels a delighted catch in his throat when he hears Amy's voice. "Thank God you're all right," he says. "How are the girls doing?"

"They're fine," says Amy, sounding relieved. "Your daughters weathered their first tornado without even crying. Mom is here with me. Dad's in another shelter. How are Harley and Muff?"

"Harley and Muff? Aren't they with you?"

"No!" She's alarmed.

"Honey . . . when I got home, they weren't here . . . I was hoping that you'd changed your mind and took them with you!"

"Oh, John . . . I'm heartsick. They must have gotten scared and broke out."

"I'll go look for them as soon as I can, hon. Don't you worry. Dogs know how to survive. We'll find them. Promise. Are you staying the night with your mom?"

Amy, now crying silently, can't speak for a moment. "Yes . . . I'll stay here. Call me, please, when you find them. Call me . . . in any case."

> Drenched and shaking, Muff crawls from beneath
> the overhang. She looks in every direction . . .
> hoping against hope that she can see Harley. With
> head hung low, and frightened eyes, she begins
> to aimlessly wander among the piles of wreckage.
> Looking and looking for her mom.

When John and his friends come up from the storm cellar, they are surprised that the damage is not as great as they'd imagined. Yet, a few miles away, south of Midwest City, all the way from Moore down to Bridge Creek, there is a massive path of devastation.

Using the last hour of light before nightfall, John drives through unrecognizable neighborhoods searching for Harley and Muff, his pulse pumping fast. There are no animals in sight. Nothing but piles of wreckage, mile after mile. Every once in a while, he stops, lowers the window, and shouts, "Harley! Muff!" There's no sign of them.

Driving on to be with Amy and the girls at his in-laws' home in Harrah, John has a heavy heart as he listens to the news on the car radio. An astonished local reporter gives an update, announcing that their area has just experienced the highest tornado winds in recorded history, anywhere in America.

"A total of fifty-eight tornadoes hit the area south of Oklahoma City. The largest tornado nearly exceeded the National Weather Service measurement of EF5, the highest numerical designation for storms with winds between 261 to 318 miles an hour." Aghast, the man continues, "This one . . . the Bridge Creek–Moore tornado . . . had the highest winds on record . . . 318 miles per hour!"*

🐾　🐾　🐾

The morning after the storm is beautiful, a strange contrast to the unsightly debris strewn everywhere—particularly around ground zero. Amy and John are thankful that they missed the brunt of the storm—they profusely thank the Almighty for that—but are profoundly sad about their missing dogs. As Amy makes breakfast and feeds the babies at her mom and

---

* National Weather Service, https://www.weather.gov/oun/events-19990503-fastfacts, accessed October 26, 2019.

dad's house, she's anxious to get home to see if Harley and Muff have made their way back. "Dogs find their way back home," John repeats, trying to reassure her.

An hour later, they pull into their driveway, with hearts sinking again. The dogs are not there.

> Muff is achy and hungry. She keeps walking, looking for her mom. She smells something. Many dogs. Danger! Too late! Something quickly drops over her neck and she's wrapped into a ball by a net that smells like other dogs. A dogcatcher is pulling her . . . and she's flipped over, falling into a truck packed with other dogs . . . arriving at a big barn filled with what seems like hundreds of dogs. She smells dog food. But other dogs are fighting over it. She decides to lay low, and go hungry.

One Month Later

> Muff is weak and lonely. She misses her mother, Harley. And Amy. And she longs for the vanilla cookie smell of the babies. In this place there's a constant morbid stench. So many other dogs are worse off than she is.

Theresa Monnard's phone is ringing incessantly. After the killer tornado, friends and other pet owners formed an information network.

Over the phone, Theresa describes the dire situation for someone: "Just imagine lost animals wandering aimlessly with noplace to go, after a storm pummels them with 318-mile-an-hour winds. Even if the dogs survive, get lucky by ending up in a shelter, and even if their family is located, their home may have been wiped out, with the adults and kids now crammed into a hotel that doesn't allow pets."

Rescue centers around Oklahoma City are bursting at the seams. They desperately seek help from experienced dog owners who can temporarily house pets. Theresa is a perfect candidate, living on a twenty-acre ranch south of Oklahoma City, in Newcastle, where they breed Appaloosa horses and Dalmatian dogs.

"I've got space. We can hold some dogs, especially Dalmatians," says Theresa into the phone to a volunteer with the Oklahoma City Animal Welfare Division. He is telling her that a Dalmatian had been picked up after the storm and was being kept in a holding area.

"I'll be by shortly," she says, and hangs up.

She's an expert on the behavior patterns of Dalmatians; that they can be nervous, depressed, and highly energetic, especially after traumatic circumstances. They are not always comfort dogs. People have been telling her for some time that she ought to start a nonprofit rescue service. Given the present situation, that idea seems like a good one.

When she arrives at the holding area, Theresa's stomach turns. Too many dogs, in too small a space; too little food, water, or medical attention. She finds the Dalmatian. The pup is skinny, frightened, and guarded.

"C'mon, girl . . . I'm going to get you fixed up, and try to get you a home," says Theresa in a gentle voice. "What's your name?" Then she sees the collar. "Is it Muff? Is that your name, sweet girl?"

Theresa later discovers that Muff does not have an embedded microchip; there is no history on her, no way of knowing where she belongs. Getting a microchip is the first order of new business.

🐾 🐾 🐾

Amy and John spend every day for weeks following the tornadoes calling and visiting animal shelters and dog rescues in the Oklahoma City area. Nearly every night Amy tears up, wondering where Harley and Muff are, praying that they have survived, and that they're somewhere safe.

Two Months After the Tornadoes

A young couple with a five-year-old girl have watched the new Disney movie *101 Dalmatians*. Now the child relentlessly asks her parents for one of those spotted white dogs. Shortly after that, a photo of Muff pops up on the website of a local shelter that is working with Theresa's farm on Rock Creek Road. Theresa houses some of their dogs and, in turn, they seek to find homes for Theresa's dogs—including Muff. The couple was sent to visit the farm.

Theresa makes notes of their conversation. "The couple seem nice and their daughter is over the moon to have a Dalmatian." But Theresa has to rely on the shelter to fully check out and approve the family before releasing Muff into their care.

Yet, even after the approval comes in . . . Theresa, herself, is not 100 percent sure. She asks the family a multitude of questions and cautions them about the Dalmatian breed, explaining that "they are not the cute well-trained dogs you see in the movies." Still, the family is undaunted; they say they will provide Muff with the most perfect home.

Little does Theresa know that later on, it will be Muff's experience with that couple that provides the primary impetus for her to start the RockySpot Rescue Shelter, complete with a careful regimen of evaluation for every prospective owner.

When Theresa's Dalmatian population reached thirty-two dogs, it was time to file for 501(c)(3) status as a non-profit organization.

Six Months After the Tornadoes

Theresa receives a call from Muff's adoptive family. The woman says that Muff was hit by a car.

"What?" she says into the phone, shocked by what she's hearing.

"The vet bills for surgery are very high and we don't know how we can pay them," the woman continues, while assuring Theresa that Muff is recovering well.

Theresa—struggling with expenses herself because RockySpot Rescue's nonprofit status has not yet been finally approved—says she can't help financially, but offers to take Muff back.

Theresa, with a worried tone in her voice, repeats, "I really mean it. If you're having a hard time, we'll take Muff back."

"No . . ." the woman answers tentatively, "my daughter loves the dog."

"Well, you let me know if you change your mind, okay?"

"Okay," says the woman.

For the next eighteen months Theresa never hears from the woman again. Their number has been disconnected and apparently they have moved. She hopes everything is all right.

One and a Half Years After the Tornadoes

Amy and John continue to visit animal shelters one weekend a month, hoping against hope that they can find Harley and Muff. They always leave with disappointment.

> Muff lies in the tall grass, nearly motionless.
> She's weak and thirsty. She can see the little girl's
> plastic pool, with the green water in it. Yet, every
> time she attempts to move toward it, she's
> stopped. The chain attached to her collar is
> wrapped around a stake in the ground. She has
> no choice. Just lie there. And whine, or try to bark
> once in a while.

🐾 🐾 🐾

Now that the girls are two years old, Amy and John have purchased a larger home in Choctaw, ten miles from Midwest City, closer to Amy's parents and more suitable for raising the twins and the two new dogs that have joined the family.

The day the movers are coming to load up the household furnishings, Amy becomes worried. She tells John at breakfast, "What if a shelter is trying to reach us about Harley and Muff and they can't find us because we've moved?"

"Well, to be on the safe side, why don't you contact as many shelters as possible and give 'em our forwarding address."

"Good idea," she says, with a slight smile. "That'll keep me from nagging the movers not to scratch the furniture."

He laughs. "Gotta get to work. See you at the new house tonight."

"Bring a pizza. We'll have our first meal at our new home."

He pecks her on the cheek and leaves.

By midday, the movers have the truck almost packed up; Amy gives them the new address, then tells them she's going ahead and will meet them there.

Strapping Emerson and Preslee safely into their car seats in the back, Amy begins the ten-mile drive to their new house.

Fifteen minutes later she realizes she missed her turn into the new neighborhood and is getting frustrated, trying to find her way back. Driving down one street after another, she tries to find a street sign, to figure out where she is, to get back on course. She figures she's probably just a couple miles from their house, part of a new development, but where she is now is an older, run-down-looking neighborhood.

> Muff sniffs the air. *What's that?* She pulls at the
> chain, tightly holding her neck. She sniffs again.
> For a moment she feels hope rising within her.
> It's the smell of vanilla cookies! The babies! She
> hears a car drive by. Then . . . it's gone.

Amy wants to get out of this neighborhood. She drives past a vacant house with tall grass all around it.

🐾   🐾   🐾

Theresa receives an alarming phone call. The lady says that she lives next door to a vacant home with tall grass growing up all around it. She'd occasionally hear a dog yelping and whining. When she approached the neighbor's back-yard, she saw a Dalmatian had been left there, tied up. She explains that the poor dog's chain was wrapped around a stake and couldn't be unwound. The lady says she left the pup some food and water, but didn't know what else to do, so she called RockySpot Rescue, now listed as an official shelter in the directory.

"Give me your address. I'll be right over," says Theresa firmly into the phone.

Theresa is apprehensive as she approaches the vacant home. She walks through the tall grass, around to the backyard, and is instantly devastated by what she sees. Muff is lying on the ground, motionless. Theresa softly calls out her name as she slowly approaches. Is the dog even alive? Then, she sees the flicker of an eyelid.

"Oh, you poor baby," says Theresa, kneeling down to stroke Muff. Anger rises up within her as a sickening feeling crosses her stomach. Pressing her lips tightly together, she whispers, "How could they do this to you!"

After snapping the chain with a wire cutter, Theresa wraps Muff in a horse blanket, then gently carries her back to the truck, driving out of Choctaw. "How could they do that to you," Theresa repeats in a sweet tone to Muff . . . belying the seething anger that she is feeling raging inside.

A little more than a mile away, Amy and the toddlers are now in their new home, getting ready for Daddy to join them for their first dinner there.

For the next couple of years, whenever Amy finds herself shopping at the bigger stores in the Midwest City area, she takes the time to drive through their old neighborhood, looking for a lost Dalmatian—or two. She always says a little prayer for Muff and Harley, and sadly drives on.

Two Years After the Tornadoes

Theresa and her helpers at RockySpot Rescue nurture Muff back to health and once again she is ready to be considered for adoption.

An active couple with no children is fully checked out and approved to adopt Muff. Theresa reiterates the characteristics of Dalmatians so they'll know what to expect.

They are thrilled. They can't wait to take her home. Unfortunately, the honeymoon lasts only six months. There is a major family crisis and the couple ask Theresa if they can return Muff.

> Each time Muff is rejected, her depression gets a little deeper. Muff had really gotten to like that couple.
> And while it's nice to be with Theresa again, she still misses the people who took good care of her.

Three Years After the Tornadoes

Amy and John's daughters, Emerson and Preslee, at three and a half, are inquisitive little girls and love the family's two dogs. Yet one of their favorite movies is *101 Dalmatians*, and they frequently ask their mom to tell the story about the brown-spotted Dalmatians she used to have.

"The mommy Dalmatian was Harley, and her daughter, the puppy, was named Muff. And why was that?" The girls would make the gesture, the way Amy had taught them to, of putting on earmuffs. "Earmuffs!" they would gaily say together.

Amy likes keeping the legend of Harley and Muff alive for her children, but she also never fails to say a silent prayer that the dogs have survived.

🐾   🐾   🐾

Theresa places Muff with a third home, that of a sweet older couple, who are fully checked out and approved. They convince Theresa that the energy level of a Dalmatian will not be too much for them. To prove it, they frequently send photos of playful times on their nicely manicured lawn.

> Muff likes the friendly man and lady and expresses
> her excitement for her new home by jumping and
> running all through the house. She is certain they'll
> appreciate that.

The couple sadly phones Theresa, admitting that Muff indeed has much more energy than they'd expected. Could she take her back?

One more time Theresa nurses Muff out of a state of depression, then at the appropriate time, reopens a search for a suitable home.

Three and a Half Years After the Tornadoes

The fourth home, carefully vetted by Theresa, is a family with three loving, active children, who appear to be a good match for Muff's activity level. Their home is located in a small town with an abundant yard.

Now more cautious than ever, Theresa stops by unexpectedly whenever she's driving down the interstate. She has other volunteers doing the same. She is pleased with what she's seen until one day, talking with the owner, she's told that Muff had been shot by a neighbor.

"What?!"

Muff loved running in the big space of her new home, and one day, she bounded through a faulty gate, right onto the property next door. Uh-oh. That neighbor shouted in a mean voice. He didn't like dogs. Told her to git. But Muff decided to show him how friendly she was by running real fast through his yard.

BAM!

Ow. It hurt terribly. Something struck her backside. She went down. After a few minutes of being stunned, and just lying on the ground, she managed to crawl back toward the gate. She lay there in a collapsed state until one of the kids found her. They quickly called their parents, who ran out to see what happened. The nice veterinarian came, gave her a shot, and fixed her up. She was bandaged for several days.

Theresa grills the adoptive family. They nonchalantly say they had the bullet removed. And promise to install a proper gate to prevent Muff from reoffending the neighbor.

Theresa makes it a point to phone the family, or stop by, at least once a month, always voicing concerns about the neighbor. She reminds them that she's willing to take Muff back, any time they feel they can't keep her safe.

Unexpectedly, Theresa receives that call a short while later. One of the older kids brought home a second dog: a pit bull.

> Muff sniffs the air. *Another dog! Oh no! Another dog is right here in my house!* The dog growls at her. Then, he suddenly attacks her, biting her leg, causing her to bleed!
>
> The owner yells at the mean dog, and shoos him away. But, every successive day, Muff is greeted by a snarling dog that often attacks her ferociously. She is wounded almost every time.
>
> Then . . . *Thank goodness! Theresa's here!*

Theresa takes the call from the owner and comes right away. Recognizing that Muff is wounded by bites, she places her on the front seat of her truck, and talks to her, petting her, all the way back to RockySpot.

Six Years After the Tornadoes

Although Muff is once again nursed back to good health, her spirits are persistently low. She demonstrates no enthusiasm. Theresa worries that the pup's episodes of rejection are just too much for her.

After the last adoptive family allowed Muff to be mis-treated, Theresa tells her staff that she has drawn the line. "No more. I'm never going to let this sweet dog be pun-ished anymore."

It was nice to be back at Theresa's ranch, but Muff just doesn't feel up to running with the other dogs. Theresa has so many Dalmatians, they stretch as far as the eye can see when all sixty of them line up near the wire fence, excitedly trying to see who is coming down the long driveway.

As she lies in the pasture with butterflies fluttering all around, she remembers the good times. If she strains her memory, she can re-create mind-movies of wonderful days long ago when she romped and played tag with her mom, Harley. And she loves holding on to the image of those little babies that smelled and tasted so good . . . like vanilla cookies . . . when she licked their hands.

After several months of observing Muff's depression, one of Theresa's volunteers treads on sensitive territory. She asks if a family with nice children, giving Muff a good home, might be just the thing to get her out of her doldrums. The young volunteer braces herself for Theresa's protective response. She knows Muff is special to Theresa.

Instead Theresa is pensive. *Maybe I'm being overprotective*, she muses. "We'll think about it," she tells the young woman.

RockySpot Rescue now has an exemplary reputation, earning the respect of animal agencies and rescue services in the Oklahoma City area. RockySpot is among the first rescues to be invited to show their pups at adoption shows.

PetSmart is holding a big one for Easter weekend. With trepidation, after agonizing over the decision for days, Theresa reluctantly says it will be okay for Muff's picture to be included among the dogs that'll be offered.

🐾   🐾   🐾

Amy and John have no hope of sleeping in on Sunday morning. Not this week. It's Easter Sunday—the girls know it's a special day, and they excitedly want to know what the Easter Bunny might have brought them. They pull at their mom and dad to get up and take part in all the fun. After the girls tear through the house looking for hidden baskets with chocolate bunnies and yellow marshmallow chicks, Amy gathers everyone for breakfast. The girls are darling photo ops as they sit at the table wearing bunny ears clipped to their heads.

The phone rings. It's Amy's mom, Donna.

"Amy, guess what?" she asks her daughter.

"What, Mom?"

"Allison made a discovery," says Donna breathlessly. She's referring to Amy's youngest sister, who was visiting her parents.

"She said she wanted to look for a dog of her own, so she went online, looking at all the pups being offered for adoption this weekend at PetSmart."

Amy nods, wondering where her mother is going with this story.

"Well, here's the Godwink. I happened to walk through the room just as Allison had the picture of a dog on the computer screen. I froze!" exclaims Donna. "Amy . . . I swear . . . she was looking at Muff!"

"What?!" says Amy, bolting to her feet. "How do you know, Mom?"

"Amy, google 'PetSmart's Easter Adoption, Midwest City,' and take a look for yourself. You and I know those earmuff-like markings on that dog!"

Amy darts from the kitchen to her computer in the family room. John, curious about what is going on, follows her. The girls continue watching a TV program in the kitchen.

"What's going on?" asks John, seeing her quickly type something into the computer.

Speaking so the girls won't hear, she whispers, "Mom says there's a photo . . . of Muff . . . up for adoption."

"No way! I don't believe it. That dog couldn't have survived that tornado. I bet your mom only *thinks* she saw Muff."

Amy is now pulling up the site and scrolling through photos of dogs up for adoption. There she is! A photo of an older Dalmatian with the uniquely spotted ears that identified Muff.

Amy looks at John. "Can that be her?"

John shakes his head, twisting his mouth. "Maybe it's just another Dalmatian with the same markings." Then, addressing a different thought: "Amy, we don't have room for another dog."

"But look at her, John . . . that *could* be Muff. Humor me. Let's go see."

"Well . . . that dog does look like Muff."

They agree to just tell the girls they are going to do some shopping in Midwest City and get food for the dogs.

🐾 🐾 🐾

When they get to the store, the plan is for John to take the girls to look at other pets while Amy tries to find the rescue booth named in the screenshot printed out from the computer.

At RockySpot Rescue's booth, she holds up the dog's picture to a volunteer.

"Sorry, that dog's not available," says the lady.

"I think this is my dog," begins Amy, showing the woman a photo of Muff as a puppy.

The RockySpot volunteer appears doubtful and protective.

"We lost her in the May third tornado, six years ago . . ." continues Amy.

"The tornado?" the lady says. Amy now has the woman's attention. She again looks at the photo. "Well . . . it could be her. But this dog was not sent up here with us today. I don't know any more than that."

"Could you call? Could we visit them?"

The volunteer is soon on the phone explaining the situation. The person on the other end is apparently hesitant, then consents. The volunteer then gives Amy the name of Theresa Monnard, and the directions to get to RockySpot, the Dalmatian rescue, forty-five minutes away in New-castle, Oklahoma.

☙ ☙ ☙

Theresa wasn't expecting a call like that. After six years, someone shows up saying they are Muff's owners? She's doubtful. *What are the odds of that?* she thinks skeptically. Besides, earlier that morning, she'd already made her firm decision. She'd been up half the night with second thoughts about allowing Muff to be again considered for adoption. At the last minute she resolved that she was going to stick to her guns—and the promise she made to Muff—not to put her through another adoption process. She'd decided to pull her out of the candidates they were sending up to the dog adoption at PetSmart. *Nope . . . that sweet dog has simply been through too much for any creature to have to endure.*

Now she is dreading that these people are heading to her farm. She doesn't really want to hear some made-up sob story from well-intentioned people, like so many in the past. She vows to turn them away as soon as possible.

☙ ☙ ☙

As John turns the car onto a long dirt road from the main road to the farmhouse, Emerson and Preslee in the back seat begin shouting with excitement. All they can see are Dalmatians! They think they have been transported to the Disney studios . . . and maybe they're in the midst of making another movie!

> Muff lies listlessly a short distance back from the fence as the other dogs start making a fuss over the approaching car.

Expecting the visitors, Theresa steps out on the farmhouse porch, looking pensively at the car approaching in a cloud of dust as it slowly moves along the dirt drive.

Muff has been through too much! In her mind, Theresa repeats the statement she had made to the volunteers that morning as they were leaving for the adoption show. *I promised I would protect her and never let anyone hurt her again.*

The car pulls up. Amy gets out and walks up to the porch as John and the girls remain in the car.

"Hi, I'm Amy Collins. I called you . . . I think the Dalmatian you've offered for adoption may be our dog."

"Why do you think that?" asks Theresa almost curtly.

"Well, I have these photos of her as a puppy, taken just before the May third tornado."

Theresa looks at the photos. She shrugs. "This is a puppy. I don't know if that's her. She had no microchip when I picked her up after the storm. And, honestly . . . this dog has been through so much . . ."

In the car, Emerson and Preslee are beside themselves, wanting to get out to see the dogs, to be with their mother. "Daddy, can't we get out now?" asks Emerson. "Please, please, Daddy?" adds Preslee.

"We just need to wait till Mommy finishes talking to that lady," he replies.

"What are they talking about?" Emerson wants to know. "Is Mommy getting us a puppy, Daddy?" Preslee asks.

🐾   🐾   🐾

Theresa is laying out her rationale. "This dog was mistreated by horrible conditions after the storm. One couple chained her to a stake and left her to starve to death; in another situation she was shot by an angry neighbor and then allowed to be attacked by a pit bull. I love this dog. I don't want anything to happen to her, ever again."

Amy can feel Theresa's passion. She wasn't expecting this reception. This is clearly a woman who loves the dog and has her best interests in mind. As Theresa talks about what had happened, Amy realizes that if it *is* Muff, the dog spent much more time with Theresa over the last six years than with her; after all, *she* only had Muff for a year and a half.

"Perhaps you're right," says Amy hesitantly. "If this *is* our dog, perhaps she's better off staying here, where she's so well taken care of." She takes a step to leave.

🐾   🐾   🐾

"Girls, settle down," says John, trying to calm his daughters' unbridled enthusiasm.

"It smells like a farm here, Daddy!" says Emerson, who discovered that the back window is not on the usual child-lock position. She pokes her head out the window. Preslee joins her. The two of them are gleefully looking at all the dogs now barking back at them from the long fence.

> Muff continues to lie on the ground while all
> the other dogs display curiosity. Then . . . sniff . . .
> she smells it! She lifts her head, turns toward the
> visitors, and smells it stronger. It's the vanilla cookie
> smell! The smell of her babies!
>
> Muff leaps to her feet, dashing to the fence. At
> the gate she uncharacteristically begins crying,

howling, and jumping crazily, trying to climb
the fence!

"I'm so sorry your dog had to go through so much,"
says Amy, stepping down from the porch toward the car.
"And . . . well . . . six years is a long time."

Theresa pauses, looking directly at Amy, appreciating
her candor. Suddenly, she is drawn to the commotion at
the gate. It's Muff, jumping out of her skin, trying to get
everyone's attention. "Wha . . . what's going on?" says Theresa, looking more closely.

Amy looks at the Dalmatian that appears to want to do
backflips. "Muff, is that you?" says Amy.

Theresa's countenance suddenly brightens. "Oh, my
goodness. You called her Muff! You know her and she
knows you! She's got your scent," says Theresa, waving for
Amy to follow her.

Theresa pulls the gate open and Muff bolts . . . not to
Amy or Theresa . . . but toward the two six-year-olds! Their
dad is just letting them out.

Muff races toward them! She jumps excitedly, almost
knocking them over.

> *It's them, it's them*, thinks Muff, inhaling that sweet
> smell from years before. The babies would be older
> now . . . *but that's them. For sure!*

Now Muff recognizes Amy. She dances with joy, jumping up, running around her in circles, and barking happily.

Amy looks at Theresa. There is a pause as, mother to mother, their hearts speak through their eyes.

"That's your dog. For sure," says Theresa, struggling to hold back tears. "Go. We'll handle the paperwork later."

Amy reaches out, touches Theresa's arm, and says, "We'll take very good care of her. Promise." She walks to the car, opens the door, and turns to take one look back. She mouths the words *Thank you*.

Moments later, struggling with her emotions, Theresa feels a tear trickle down her cheek as she gazes at the back of the car slowly leaving her farm. The faces of two delighted six-year-olds hugging Muff, from either side, are looking back at her from the rear window of the departing car.

Later . . .

> Muff couldn't be happier. She sits patiently on the floor of the family room as the girls fuss over her. She is the guest of honor at their "Easter afternoon tea party." Muff can't tell what is happening, but she

knows something is on her head while something else covers her back.

Click. Amy takes a charming photo of Muff, wearing bunny ears and a cape, as the girls sip their imaginary tea.

Yep. This is the dog's life I've always wanted.

CONCLUSION

God and Dog Work as a Team

We observed at the outset that DOG mirrors GOD:

- The three letters are the same.
- They both communicate with us without using the spoken word.
- They provide enormous comfort and protection.
- Dogs are God's furry friendly agents on earth.

From the stories in this book, we have learned that dogs have a definite *purpose* in God's grand plan for us:

- Louise's dog, Spotty, and Landon's cleft-palate pup, Bogart, were *comfort* dogs.

- Trixie and Sasha were *protector* dogs . . . Trixie
  protecting Bill the soldier and, later, his child,
  while Sasha warned Nana that the house was on fire.
- Two huskies were *detectives*: Sierra was a cancer-
  finding canine, and Hunter a gas-smelling pup.
  Both saved lives.

Muff demonstrated that dogs have *purpose* in a different
manner. Her dogwink adventure through twists and turns
to sometimes dark and scary places was a microcosm of so
many of our lives.

You may think your life is random, like a twig floating
downstream to destinations unknown. But it isn't. Inside
your DNA is a grand plan just for you. You have *purpose*.
A destiny.

True, God allows you free will to have your hands on
the steering wheel most of the way through life. You can
go too fast, too slow, or leave the main highway altogether,
ending up on the back roads of life.

But a time will come when He takes the wheel, and
pulls you safely over to a sudden stop. That's usually when
you realize that you should have let Him do the driving all
along. His map is better than yours.

That's also a good time to reflect on all the crossroads
in your past when He was communicating directly to you

through Godwinks and divine alignment; He did that with Bullet, the dog who was saved by his owners to later save their baby's life. As well as Ruby, who was saved through the efforts of Pat, and later became the hero saving Pat's son.

In your past, you may recall that you were divinely aligned to be at the right place at the right time for you to meet the person who led you to something that changed your life, perhaps to a job that opened the door to your career. Or when you "just happened" to meet the very person God had in mind to be your perfect mate. You realize now that if you had arrived five minutes sooner or later, you would never have met.

Every divinely aligned encounter was a Godwink. If a friendly, comforting, protective pup was involved, it was a dogwink.

So, as you greet your favorite four-legged friend today, appreciate that your dog is a special messenger from God, helping to inspire and nudge you along your paths to achieve your *purpose* . . . your destiny.

Remember, you and your watchdog are always on His GPS . . . God's Positioning System.